TAKE PART
Speaking Canadian English

to fire someone — to dismiss somebody from a job

(to quit — (Voluntary leaving from a job),

(to hire — to employ a new person

TAKE PART
Speaking Canadian English

Lucia Pietrusiak Engkent   Karen P. Bardy

Prentice-Hall Canada Inc., Scarborough, Ontario

Canadian Cataloguing in Publication Data

Engkent, Lucia Pietrusiak, 1955-
    Take part: speaking Canadian English

Includes index.
ISBN 0-13-882929-2

1. English language—Canada—Textbooks for
second language learners.* 2. English language—
Spoken English—Canada. 3. Canadianisms (English).*
I. Bardy, Karen P., 1954—   II. Title.

PE1128.E53 1986   428.3'4   C85-099755-0

Prentice-Hall Inc., Englewood Cliffs, New Jersey
Prentice-Hall International, Inc., London
Prentice-Hall of Australia, Pty., Sydney
Prentice-Hall of India Pvt., Ltd., New Delhi
Prentice-Hall of Japan, Inc., Tokyo
Prentice-Hall of Southeast Asia (Pte.) Ltd., Singapore
Editora Prentice-Hall do Brasil Ltda., Rio de Janeiro
Prentice-Hall Hispanoamericana, S.A., Mexico
Whitehall Books Limited, Wellington, New Zealand

Production editor: Monica Schwalbe
Design: Steven Boyle
Illustrations: Tami Hadley
Production: Sheldon Fischer
Typesetting: CompuScreen Typesetting Ltd.

ISBN 0-13-882929-2

Manufactured in Canada by Alger Press

2 3 4 5 AP 90 89 88

Contents

Preface

Take Part: Speaking Canadian English focuses on the language and culture of everyday Canadian life. It has been designed to meet the needs of adult intermediate students, especially those who have a good grasp of formal English but have difficulty with the informal spoken language. The book offers insights into the way the language is spoken everyday and gives students the opportunity to practise speaking on a variety of topics. In addition, cultural information helps prepare students for social life in Canada.

Take Part can be used either on its own for conversation courses or as a supplementary text for multi-skill and intensive courses. It was developed in a forty-hour intermediate conversation course for adults, many of whom were foreign students or new immigrants.

Conversational English
Register, the language appropriate to a particular context, is an important part of language use. It is, however, often neglected in language teaching. There is a general tendency to smooth over register variations and homogenize the language. Although some textbooks do mark expressions as formal or informal, the actual differences between the registers are rarely explored. As a result, students often make register errors in their speech or writing. *Take Part* focuses on the conversational register of everyday English and explains what characterizes it and how it is different from more formal English. Because of this focus, there are no writing assignments in the text.

Informal conversational English is often very difficult for students to understand and use correctly. What language learners hear native speakers saying often does not conform to the formal descriptions of English found in textbooks. And with the ever-changing nature of language, students become even more confused. Even if students do not use certain colloquialisms in their speech, they need a thorough understanding of the forms and the principles involved.

One of the problems in dealing with conversational English is the question of a standard. Where do we draw the line between standard colloquial English and non-standard English, or between idiom and slang? What do we consider a vulgarism and what is grammatical "pickiness"?

As teachers and writers, we have had to draw the line ourselves. Others may disagree with us. For example, we have used the frequently heard, but technically ungrammatical, "here's" and "there's" with plural subjects—aiming for a standard conversational style of English. Forms that would be inappropriate in formal situations are marked as colloquial or slang.

By treating formal and informal English as distinct varieties, teachers can explain to the students that what they hear native speakers say in conversation is correct in that situation, but does not belong in an essay. Some students see language in absolutes—black or white, right or wrong. Colloquial English is a living, changing language; forms that are considered non-standard today may gradually become accepted. Both teachers and students must accept the forms in common use and yet be aware of factors of social acceptability in language; we cannot move to extremes and simply follow whatever forms a native speaker may use.

Organization
Take Part: Speaking Canadian English is divided into sixteen units that deal with topics of everyday conversation. The units focus on such themes as health and fitness, adult education, leisure activities, government, and travel and tourism. Various linguistic and cultural aspects of each theme are explored. Depending on the interest and needs of the students, each unit may take two or more hours to complete.

The units do not have to be studied sequentially, since the text does not depend on a gradation of structures or vocabulary. There is, however, a sense of progression in the text. The organization is thematic. Early units treat topics such as introductions and casual small talk, while later units explore more complex subjects such as the Canadian political structure. The text ends with a unit on a particular type of conversation, telephone calls.

This type of organization allows each unit to stand on its own; the teacher can choose and order the lessons according to the needs and interests of a particular class. The thematic organization means that each unit can lead to a further exploration of the topic in a wider context and that it can be integrated into existing ESL curricula.

Each unit follows essentially the same pattern: dialogues and texts introduce the topic, language notes follow up on structures and expressions in the dialogues, a culture note explains other aspects of the theme, and the additional vocabulary prepares the students to deal with the discussion topics, activities and assignments at the end of the unit. Since there is a great deal of material and activities, teachers are encouraged to make selections appropriate to the needs and interests of the particular class. In one unit, the class may do a number of role-plays; in another, they may have a discussion or debate on the topic.

Considering the wide variety of ESL teaching situations in Canada, we have tried to leave teachers and students a variety of options. Not only will the needs and interests of the students influence many of the teacher's choices, but the time and facilities available will also determine what is actually done in the classroom and how it is done. Therefore, many of the activities are left open-ended, ready for the teacher's specifications. Some of the material can also be used for self-study by the students.

Dialogues

The theme of each chapter is introduced by dialogues that illustrate typical conversations on the subject at hand and provide a context for many idiomatic expressions and different vocabulary items. Each dialogue provides models for informal conversation and stimulates further discussion.

Vocabulary notes are found in the margins next to the dialogues. These explain, for the most part, idiomatic words and expressions or unusual uses of words. Vocabulary items which may prove difficult for the students, but which have straightforward dictionary definitions, are generally not explained in the notes.

There is no continuing cast of characters in the dialogues; rather, characters are given a variety of common English first names. In this way, the names are part of the vocabulary offered in the text. Students can learn the pronunciation of names, whether a name is generally for a male or female, and some short forms of common names.

A discussion section follows each dialogue and includes comprehension questions, discussion top-

ics, and class activities. Rather than memorizing a particular dialogue, students are encouraged to practise role-play variations.

In addition to the dialogues, other texts, such as broadcast announcements and prose passages, are sometimes used to introduce the topic. These also include vocabulary notes and discussion questions.

Language Notes

The language notes are based on examples in the dialogues and focus on features of informal English. Thus, instead of following a structural syllabus, we have let the material itself dictate which structures and forms will be explored. The language notes follow up on forms and expressions used in the dialogues and explain or expand on them. There are four main kinds of language notes: notes on grammatical structures, pronunciation, idioms, and functions.

It is assumed that students at this level will have an understanding of basic English grammar. The grammar-based language notes, therefore, are brief descriptions. Some review structures that the students have studied, but the notes may look at these structures in a different light—in the context of conversational usage. The notes highlight the differences between formal and informal English, especially where these differences may mean that rules of formal grammar are "broken". As a result, *Take Part* is not a grammar text, but it does include a "mini-grammar" of informal English as it is used in everyday conversation. For example, the language note on tag questions focuses on their conversational function and their intonation patterns.

The pronunciation notes focus mainly on stress and intonation. Notes on idioms clarify confusing sets of idioms, showing a pattern where possible. Functional language notes show how certain forms are used for specific functions.

Culture Notes

The culture notes either focus on a particular aspect of a topic or help to add ideas to the general discussion. They do not explain "rules of behaviour", but offer some insights into the attitudes, customs, and lifestyles of Canadians.

There are no notes and questions directly accompanying the culture notes. A general class discussion should clear up any comprehension difficulties. As well, the last sections of the unit— Additional Vocabulary, Discussion Topics, Activities, and Assignments—follow up on many of the issues raised in the culture notes.

Additional Vocabulary

A section on additional vocabulary following the culture note offers words and expressions related to the topic which may be of use to the students in the discussion and activities. The teacher is free to omit or add to the vocabulary items.

Discussion Topics

A wide variety of discussion topics are given for each unit. Again the teacher can choose those particularly relevant to the class. They function simply as conversation starters. Some bring up controversial issues; others invite the students to share their own experiences. The goal is to encourage students to talk about matters which interest them.

Activities

The suggested class activities in each unit include role-plays, debates, and group work. The teacher can add specifications to the activity to fit the time and facilities available. For example, the teacher can determine the number of items that a group must list or the exact situation and length of a role-play dialogue. While teachers will be familiar with most types of activities suggested, different ways of structuring the activities are suggested in the Instructor's Manual.

Assignments

Suggested assignments at the end of each unit give students the opportunity to pursue some of the topics on their own. The assignments require the students to try out what they have learned in actual conversation, to do independent research, and to reflect on the material studied and their own experiences.

Instructor's Manual

The teacher's manual accompanying *Take Part* focuses on practical suggestions. The manual contains teaching strategies and hints on adapting the material to a particular class.

The role of the teacher in *Take Part* is a facilitative one, in that he or she focuses on the students and integrates the vocabulary and skills that the students bring to class with the new information introduced in the course. The teacher can help the students be comfortable in conversation by encouraging participation in a variety of informal settings. Through organizing role-plays, the teacher can help the students practise conversations similar to those they will encounter outside the classroom. Thus, the students will become more assertive and confident in expressing themselves.

Cassette

A cassette audio tape is available to accompany *Take Part*. The tape includes all dialogues from the text, as well as the news and weather reports, and the commercials (from units fourteen, two, and fifteen, respectively). The pronunciation-based language notes can be found on the tape with their exercises and example sentences; students can repeat the sentences after they hear them. The tape also includes additional dialogues, one per unit, that can be used as listening comprehension exercises. The transcript of the tape, including the additional dialogues, is printed in the instructor's manual with suggestions for use.

Acknowledgements

This text was class-tested at the English Language Program, Faculty of Extension, University of Alberta. We would like to thank the staff and students—especially Isabel Kent Henderson, Simone Devlin, Rosalie Banko, and Ruth Pearce for their invaluable help.

The work of the staff at Prentice-Hall Canada is also greatly appreciated. We would especially like to acknowledge Monica Schwalbe (Production Editor), Marta Tomins (Project Editor), and Terry Woo (Acquisitions Editor).

For their comments on the manuscript, we would like to thank Barbara Bowers (Vancouver Community College), Gail Gaffney (Algonquin College), David Levy (McGill University), Ann McIlroy (Seneca College), and Patricia Raymond (University of Ottawa).

As well, a very special thank you to Garry Engkent and Ken Coomber for their contributions and support.

one

Getting Acquainted

THE NEW CO-WORKER

take over a job—fill a position after someone has left it

how do you do—an expression used to acknowledge an introduction; note that it is not a question

show someone around—take someone on a tour, act as a guide

terminal—computer terminal

co-worker—colleague, fellow worker

give you a hand—(colloquial) help you

get the hang of it—(colloquial) get used to it

learn the ropes—(colloquial) learn how things work

Terry: Mrs. Simmons, do you have a minute?

Janet: Certainly, Terry.

Terry: I just want you to meet Susan Peterson. She'll be **taking over** Jeffrey's old job. Susan, this is Janet Simmons, the head of our accounting division.

Susan: Pleased to meet you.

Janet: **How do you do**. Did you start today?

Susan: Yes, I did. Terry has been kind enough to **show me around** the office.

Janet: I'm sure you'll like it here...

Terry: And your desk is over here. You'll be using this **terminal**. Eric, meet your new **co-worker**, Susan Peterson. Susan, this is Eric McKee.

Eric: Hi.

Susan: Hi.

Terry: Eric can **give you a hand** with the computer until you get used to it. It's different from the one you were using at Gowans', isn't it?

Susan: A bit. But I'm sure it won't take long to **get the hang of it**.

Eric: No problem. It doesn't take long to **learn the ropes** around here. It seems like just yesterday that I was a trainee myself...

Terry: Oh no, if Eric is going to start reminiscing, I think I'll just move along.

Susan: (laughs) Thanks for all your help, Terry.

Terry: Don't mention it.

Discussion

1. Are these introductions formal or informal? Why are Janet and Eric introduced differently?

2. Do you think Susan and Mrs. Simmons shook hands? Did Susan and Eric shake hands? Why or why not?

3. What do you find different about the way Canadians greet people and introduce each other from the way people do so in your culture?

4. Are you good at remembering names and faces? What is a good way to remember someone's name after an introduction?

5. In small groups, practise making various introductions in different situations. Discuss levels of formality required. For example:

   (a) introduce fellow students to each other
   (b) introduce a boss (or teacher) to your spouse
   (c) introduce your family to a co-worker

TENANT TALK

Tenant 1: (looking into his mailbox) **Hmmph!** Empty again!

Tenant 2: Better than what I have—bills, bills, bills.

Tenant 1: Depressing, **eh**?

Tenant 2: Hey, did you hear the talk about rent increases?

Tenant 1: What, again?

Tenant 2: That's how it goes. The landlords have the **upper hand** right now because of the low **vacancy rate**.

Tenant 1: Even if you can find another place—with the cost of moving and all—it's better to **stay put**.

Tenant 2: Trapped like rats in a cage. . . . Maybe a couple of laps around the track'll make me feel better.

Tenant 1: You jog?

Tenant 2: Yeah. I'm off to the field house now.

Tenant 1: Where's that? I've been looking for an indoor track for weather like this.

Tenant 2: It's at the sports centre on Main. You don't need a membership. **You wanna** come along and try it out?

Tenant 1: Sure—I could use some exercise. Hey, by the way, my name's Craig McLeod.

Tenant 2: (shaking hands) Tom Brewster. Why don't you go grab your **gear** and I'll meet you out front?

Tenant 1: Great, I'll just be a second.

Hmmph!—exclamation of disgust

eh—interjection considered characteristic of Canadian English

upper hand—the advantage, better position

vacancy rate—percentage of rental accommodations that are empty

stay put—(colloquial) stay in one place

you wanna—spoken reduction of "you want to"

gear—equipment

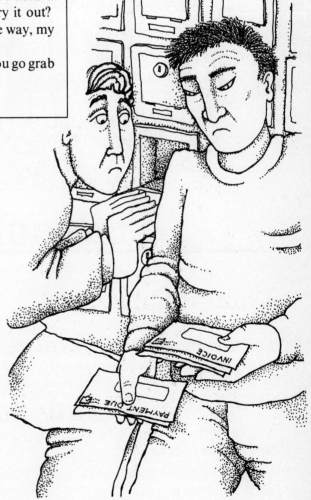

Discussion

1. How is this introduction different from those in "The New Co-worker"?

2. Do you think Craig and Tom have spoken to each other before? What kind of contact would they have had? Why do you think so?

3. In pairs and small groups, develop and role play short dialogues between people who have had some casual contact, illustrating various aspects of small talk.

Examples:

(a) a group of classmates or co-workers at a party

(b) parents at their children's school

(c) people talking before their swimming class

(d) people talking in a grocery store

(e) neighbours talking outside their homes

WAITING FOR THE BUS

Cold enough for you?—
(rhetorical question) implies that it is indeed very cold and no one would want it any colder

pay hike—increase in wages or salary, from the verb "to hike" meaning "to raise"

Stranger 1:	**Cold enough for you?**
Stranger 2:	Sure is. Can't get much colder.
Stranger 1:	At least the buses are running again.
Stranger 2:	(looks at his watch) Running late, you mean.
Stranger 1:	That **pay hike** the drivers got sure hasn't improved service.
Stranger 2:	Ah, here it comes now.

Discussion

1. What happened recently to the buses?
2. Practise starting conversations with someone standing next to you at a bus stop or in a line-up. Think of similar situations in which to start conversations. What expressions might you use?

LANGUAGE NOTES

Contractions

Contractions are used in informal standard English. The uncontracted forms are used in writing, in formal speech, and for emphasis in spoken English. "I can not do it," for example, is more emphatic than "I can't do it."

In positive statements, contractions are made with the verb *to be* and with the auxiliary verbs *have, had, will,* and *would.*

> *to be*—I'm, you're, he's, she's, it's, we're, they're
> *to have*—I've, you've, he's, she's, it's, we've, they've

> *will*—I'll, you'll, he'll, she'll, it'll, we'll, they'll
> *had & would*—I'd, you'd, he'd, she'd, it'd, we'd, they'd

Note that the contractions for *had* and *would* are the same. The same contracted form is also used for the third person singular of *to be* and *to have*. The form of the main verb indicates which verb is meant.

> She's been here before. (has)
> She's working very hard. (is)

> After I'd seen him, I found the book. (had)
> I'd go there if I could. (would)

In conversational English, contractions can also be made with nouns.

> The doctor'll be here soon. (will)
> John's going to be late again. (is)

Non-native speakers often find contractions difficult to pronounce and many simply avoid using them. While it is not necessary to use contractions (except in some cases, such as in tag questions), it is important to know how they are pronounced. Contractions reduce the sound of the verb so much that it is often indistinguishable. In a form such as "I'd better," the contracted verb form sometimes drops entirely and the phrase sounds like "I better." The pronoun is pronounced together with the contracted verb form as one word. Try pronouncing the following combinations of words. They should rhyme.

I'm—time	I'll—mile
you're—sure	you'll—tool
he's, she's—please	he'll, she'll, we'll—feel
it's—bits	it'll—little
we're—fear	they'll—fail
they're—there	I'd—ride
I've—five	you'd—rude
you've—move	he'd, she'd, we'd—feed
we've—leave	it'd—fitted
they've—save	they'd—made

Practise the contractions in the dialogues and in the following sentences:

1. I'd say he'd seen her somewhere before.
2. It'll be a long time before you hear that again.
3. They're staying at my place for the weekend.
4. I've got to go now. Tom'll be coming soon.
5. It'd be better if you'd stay.
6. But Marion's not here yet.
7. I'll be seeing you.
8. It's sad that she's leaving so soon.
9. We've always wanted to go to Paris.
10. I should've left earlier. I'm going to be late.

To Get

The verb *to get* is one of the most frequently used verbs in informal, spoken English. (Over-use of the verb should be avoided in writing.) Here are the main uses:

to receive, obtain
> That pay hike the drivers got sure hasn't improved service.
> He got a new car last week.
> I just got a letter from my friend in Brazil.

to become
> Can't get much colder.
> David got sick after the trip.
> He's always looking for a way to get rich quick.

to arrive at, reach
> How do you get to Union Station?
> I had so much other work to do that I couldn't get to that report.

to have (with the contraction of "have"; informal)
> You've got five minutes to catch that bus.
> I've got to go now.
> Susan's got a new job.

with prepositions forming two-word verbs
> You'll *get along* fine here. (do, manage, succeed)
> He *got up* late this morning. (arose, got out of bed)
> I don't know what you're *getting at*. (suggesting, saying in an indirect way)

There are many idiomatic expressions formed with the verb *to get* and prepositions. These expressions are often difficult to learn, especially since each two-word verb formed may have several different meanings. For example:

> If you want to *get on* in the world, you'll have to dress well. (succeed, make progress)
> Wait till I *get* my coat *on*. (get dressed in, put on)
> It's *getting on* so I'd better go. (becoming late)

Read each of the following sentences. Can you determine which meaning of *to get* is being used?

1. Yesterday Jake got a letter from home.
2. She's got a funny way of greeting people.
3. The nights got colder as Thanksgiving approached.
4. The students got in late last night from their ski trip.
5. "Get on with the job," James yelled at his son.

CULTURE NOTE

Generally, Canadians are informal and polite in their everyday conversations. The rules for casual politeness vary with the social situation, but a few basic suggestions may be helpful.

Canadians prefer to be on a first-name basis with acquaintances. However, a title (such as Mr., Mrs., Miss, or Ms.) with a last name is often used when a person is addressing an employer, a teacher, a client, an older person, or a stranger in formal situations. A first-name basis may then be suggested by the person with more authority ("Call me Bob"). In Canada, first names are used less frequently than in the United States, but more frequently than in Britain. Calling someone by a last name without a title, however, is more common in Britain than in North America, where it is considered too abrupt. Here a last name alone can be used as a term of reference, not address. For example, we are more likely to say "Why don't you talk to Johnson about it?" than "I was wondering if you could help me with something, Johnson."

Calling a man "Sir," or a woman "Miss" or "Ma'am," is done only in certain circumstances. Salesclerks, waiters, and others who serve the public address customers in this way. These forms are also used to get someone's attention ("Excuse me, sir. You dropped your hat."). They are traditional terms of respect, but are used less frequently today.

When introductions take place, shaking hands is customary; but much depends on the formality of the situation and on individual preference. Handshakes are firm and brief. In conversations, Canadians generally do not touch each other as casually and frequently as people in other cultures do. They also prefer a greater distance between each other in conversation than that found in

other cultures. Here, a one-metre conversational distance is usual. Any closer than this, and a person may feel uncomfortable and uneasy.

Eye contact is another important factor in conversation. Looking away may be considered a sign of dishonesty, boredom, or poor manners. On the other hand, staring, or looking too intently, may make a person feel uncomfortable.

In casual conversation, many Canadians also tend to avoid direct personal questions. Often such questions are phrased indirectly or vaguely (for instance, "Do you live around here?" instead of "Where do you live?"). Usually, when a subject of a personal nature is brought up, information is volunteered rather than asked for directly. In Canada, questions that can be considered too personal are those concerning age, religion, personal political beliefs, salary, and prices paid for items. When personal questions are asked, they are phrased very carefully.

Strangely enough, Canadians often begin conversations without exchanging names first. This practice can be awkward when two people who have been speaking to one another for some time do not know each other's name. In these cases, one speaker will often give his or her name ("By the way, I'm Jane Wilson") and expect the other to do likewise. Asking "What is your name?" is considered abrupt in conversation; a person is more likely to ask the question indirectly (for instance, "I'm sorry, but I didn't catch your name").

The guidelines for social conversations are often difficult to learn. There are no written rules and the different factors of each situation must be taken into account. The degree of formality often varies. Careful observation of native speakers is often the best way to learn how language is used.

Additional Vocabulary

conversation piece—object that serves as a topic of conversation because it is unusual

ice-breaker—topic or activity with which to start a conversation; something to "break the ice" between strangers

shop talk—conversation about job-related activities in a social situation

small talk—informal, trivial conversation between casual acquaintances

Informal greetings:
How's it going?
What've you been up to?
What's new?
Where have you been lately? I haven't seen you for a long time.

Discussion Topics

1. Discuss your own observations of small talk among Canadians. Where, when, and how do Canadians usually start a conversation? What do they talk about?
2. What topics might you discuss at a party? What topics would it be best to avoid?
3. What do you think is a good way to meet people?
4. In a group, how would you draw out someone who is shy? What questions might you ask to start a conversation?
5. What expressions do you often hear in casual conversations, greetings, and introductions?

Activities

1. In small groups, get to know your classmates through introductions and small talk. Discuss your experiences in Canada, sports you enjoy, your favourite foods, or other topics. Change groups often enough so that everyone has a chance to meet.
2. Think of situations in which you have had difficulty talking to someone at a first meeting. In small groups, discuss these situations with your classmates and try to come up with suggestions for dealing with them.

Assignments

1. Start a friendly conversation with someone you don't know very well and report to the class on your experience.
2. Make a list of differences that are apparent in casual conversations of different cultures.
3. Identify conversational taboos of various cultures. It is a conversational taboo in Canada, for example, to inquire about an individual's salary.

two
Weather Watch

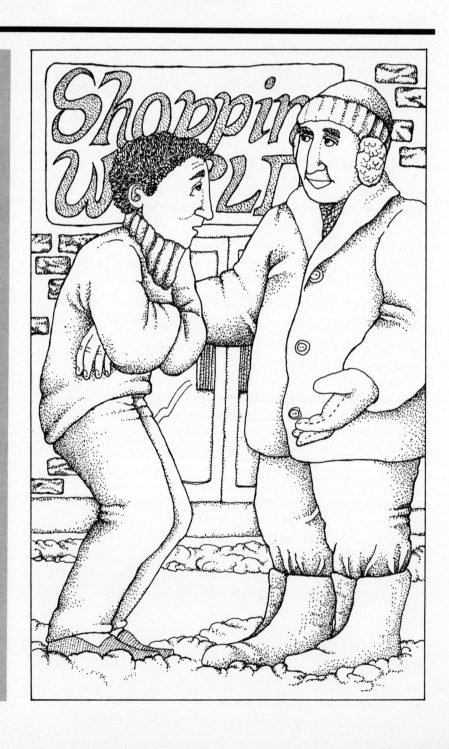

WINTER WEAR

(walking into a shopping mall)

Dave: Brrrr. It's cold out there!

Brad: Yeah, but **no wonder** you're cold. That sweater doesn't look heavy enough for this weather.

Dave: It's not too bad. It hasn't been as cold as I expected.

Brad: We haven't really **hit** winter yet. Wait till January—this is practically **balmy**.

Dave: You're right. I'll need a winter coat and some boots.

Brad: You'd better **get a move on** . . . There's a sale on in that store. Let's take a look.

Dave: How about something like this?

Brad: I'm not sure a ski jacket will be warm enough. Try a **parka**—maybe **down-filled**. These are all waterproof. Layers of clothing are warmer—the air in between acts as insulation.

Dave: How about these gloves?

Brad: Sure. And here's a **tuque** and a scarf.

Dave: All that?

Brad: (laughs) Those are just the basics—not to mention the boots.

Dave: I guess you can't **take winter lightly** here!

no wonder—(idiomatic) it's not surprising

hit—(colloquial) reached, arrived at

balmy—mild, warm

get a move on—(colloquial) be quick, hurry up

parka—a hip-length heavy coat with a hood, first worn in arctic regions

down-filled—filled with soft, fluffy feathers (down) from waterfowl (ducks, geese)

tuque—(also spelled "toque") knitted, close-fitting hat without a brim

take something lightly—(idiomatic) to treat something as not serious

Discussion

1. Describe Dave and Brad. Do you think they are young or old? What is the relationship between them? Where do you think they are from?
2. Modify the dialogue so that two people in a shopping mall are discussing the purchase of other winter clothing or equipment (e.g., skis, snow tires, children's snowsuits, fur coat, sled, skates, snowmobile). Role play the new dialogue for the class.
3. What advice would you give someone preparing for his or her first winter in Canada?

WEATHER REPORTS

take heart—(idiomatic) be encouraged, cheer up
picnickers—people going on a picnic
heat wave—long period of very hot weather
record temperature—highest or lowest temperature recorded for that day
nose dive—(colloquial) sudden, sharp drop
Indian summer—period of mild weather that occurs in the fall
traveller's advisory—warning to travellers
pile-up—collision involving several cars
sanding operations—icy roads are covered with sand to improve traction

"**Take heart**, all you golfers and **picnickers**—the rain is not here to stay. We can expect clearing skies tomorrow and a warm and sunny weekend. Highs should be around 28 degrees with lows near 18."

"There's no relief in sight from the hot, humid weather. Day 9 of the **heat wave** resulted in another **record temperature**. The record of 33 degrees for July 17 in 1943 was broken by today's high of 34. Local stores are reportedly unable to keep up with the demand for fans and air conditioners."

"Temperatures took a sharp **nose dive** last night and it looks like the end of the **Indian summer** we've been enjoying. There is a frost warning tonight as we expect even cooler temperatures. Low tonight –2, high Wednesday 10 degrees."

"The weather office has issued a **traveller's advisory** today as the freezing rain makes driving conditions hazardous. A six-car **pile-up** has closed Highway 2 southbound 50 kilometres from the city. **Sanding operations** are continuing and work crews are expected to be out all night. If you must be on the roads, be extremely careful."

Discussion

1. Which seasons do the weather reports describe? Describe the weather at the time of the reports in your own words.
2. Listen to taped weather reports in class. Summarize the reports and list the weather vocabulary used.
3. In small groups, compose brief weather reports for different times of the year. Perform these reports for the class.
4. Compare the weather at various times of year in your native country with that in Canada. Discuss the differences with the class.

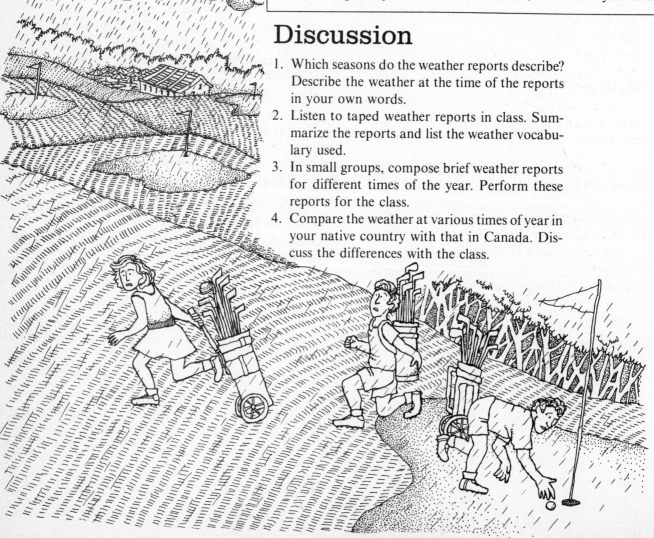

LANGUAGE NOTES

Negative Contractions

Auxiliary verbs are often contracted with *not* in speech. The verb *to be* has two possible contractions with *not* (*he isn't, he's not*) for all persons except the first person singular. For the auxiliaries *have, will, would,* and *had,* it is preferable to use the auxiliary contracted with *not* rather than the auxiliary contracted with the pronoun (*I haven't* rather than *I've not*).

> *to be*—aren't, isn't (there is no contraction for *am* with *not*; "aren't I" is the form used in questions, "I'm not" is the only other form used)
> *to be* (past)—wasn't, weren't
> *to have*—haven't, hasn't
> *to do*—don't, doesn't

The following forms of auxiliary verbs + *not* remain the same for each person:

> will not—won't
> did not—didn't
> had not—hadn't
> would not—wouldn't
> should not—shouldn't
> could not—couldn't
> cannot—can't
> must not—mustn't

The forms *needn't, oughtn't,* and *mightn't* also exist but are not usually used in Canadian English.

Negative contractions are pronounced with no vowel sounds between the final sound of the verb, the *n,* and the *t.* Some of the resulting consonant clusters are difficult for non-native speakers to pronounce. The nasal sound of the *n* should provide the bridge between a final consonant of the verb and the *t.*

Practise pronouncing the contractions in the dialogues and in the following sentences:

1. Don't worry, we won't be late.
2. I don't think it'll be warm tomorrow.
3. You'd better not take your winter tires off yet.
4. She doesn't mind if it's not sunny.
5. I can't go out without my umbrella and rubber boots.
6. It isn't raining that hard!
7. He wouldn't've been late if he'd had the car.
8. I haven't had a chance to finish that yet.
9. We weren't expecting company.
10. He wasn't back yet so I couldn't go.

Stress of Auxiliary Verbs

Auxiliary verbs are not usually stressed in English, except for emphasis. Vowel sounds in unstressed syllables are reduced; they often become the sound schwa /ə/ or drop entirely. *Can,* for example, is often pronounced /kn/ in a sentence. However, auxiliary verbs with negative contractions do receive a stress. This stress pattern serves to signal the negative form. Improper stress on the auxiliary verb can result in a misunderstanding as to whether the positive or negative is meant, especially for the forms of *can.*

> I *can* go. (the auxiliary is pronounced /kn/ and the pitch rises on the main verb)
> I *can't* go. (the auxiliary is pronounced /kæn/ and the pitch rises on the auxiliary verb)

CULTURE NOTE

Weather is probably one of the most popular topics for small talk among Canadians. After all, it's a safe topic since no one can be blamed for it.

Canadian weather is so changeable, from season to season, and from day to day, that there is always something to be said about it. There are also many climatic differences among the various regions of Canada. When it is a mild, wet day in Vancouver, it can be –20 degrees and snowing in central Ontario.

Some people think that climate influences the personality of a people. It is generally thought that people from northern climates are cold and unfriendly, and that people from southern regions are hot-tempered and passionate.

Many people in the world think of Canada as a land of cold and snow; they are unprepared for the extremes of weather that Canadians experience. There are hot summers as well as cold winters. Many Canadians take pride in their ability to cope with adverse weather conditions.

Even so, Canadians often grumble about the weather. Many seek to escape winter's cold with holidays in warm southern climates. Most do enjoy the changing seasons, however, and would find life extremely dull in a region where the weather changes little. Most Canadians enjoy the all-too-brief summer and the incredibly beautiful autumn; they hope for a white Christmas and feel the joy of each new spring.

Additional Vocabulary

blizzard—severe snowstorm
hail—rounded lumps of ice that may fall during thunderstorms
downpour—heavy rainfall
drizzle—very light rainfall
chilly—rather cold, unpleasantly cold
wind chill factor—the chilling effect of wind in combination with low temperatures
slush—partly melted, wet snow
to winterize—to prepare (usually a car or a building) for winter
drifting snow—snow that is blown about and heaped up by the wind
it's raining cats and dogs—(idiomatic) it's raining very hard

Weather-inspired idioms:

to be under the weather—not feeling well
to weather the storm—to pass safely through the storm or, figuratively, through any adverse conditions
it never rains but it pours—(proverb) misfortunes rarely come alone
to shoot the breeze—to talk about trivial matters, to make small talk
windfall—literally, fruit blown down by the wind; figuratively, an unexpected stroke of good luck

Discussion Topics

1. How do you think the weather affects people?
2. Do you think different cultures have different personalities because of climate?
3. What would be the ideal climate for you?
4. What is your cure for the January "blahs" (the dull feeling that comes with mid-winter)?
5. Which season or month do you enjoy most? Why?

Activities

1. With the aid of a map, role play a national TV weather report.
2. In pairs, develop and role play a dialogue about the weather of the day.

Assignments

1. Keep track of the number of times people start conversations with small talk about the weather. Keep a record of different expressions. Report to the class any interesting findings.
2. Make a list of weather terms and idioms not included in the vocabulary lists.
3. Find out about the climate in different regions of Canada.

three
The Workplace

13

NINE TO FIVE

to get me down—(colloquial) to depress or discourage me
grind—long, hard work or study
to get to me—to affect or bother me
thrive—grow well, prosper, flourish
pussycat—(slang) gentle person
Attila the Hun—a Mongol conqueror in the fifth century, used today metaphorically for a demanding, aggressive person
on the road—travelling, usually for business
lateral transfer—transfer to a position of the same rank, not a promotion
try my hand at—(idiomatic) try
gripe—(colloquial) complain
there's—contraction of "there is" often used with a plural predicate in informal speech, but incorrect in formal English

Grace: You know, Hillary, my job is really starting **to get me down**. I just don't feel inspired about it anymore.

Hillary: I thought you liked working in the lab.

Grace: I did. I thought it was great stuff in school. But now with the daily **grind** of the nine to five routine, it's starting **to get to me**. We always have a deadline to meet. Rush, rush, rush. My supervisor's so demanding.

Hillary: A lot of jobs are stressful, and didn't you once tell me you **thrived** on pressure?

Grace: Maybe I'm getting old. I feel like I'm under too much strain these days.

Hillary: Have you looked into changing jobs?

Grace: Well, I did notice one of the other departments is looking for a technician. But the supervisor there makes mine look like a **pussycat**. They call him **Attila the Hun** Atkinson.

Hillary: (chuckles) It's a good thing I don't see my boss that often. He's always **on the road**.

Grace: The possibilities for a **lateral transfer** seem pretty slim right now. And lab technicians aren't in demand at other companies. Actually, I'd like to **try my hand at** something completely different.

Hillary: So, why don't you?

Grace: Then my two years in college would be wasted!

Hillary: Why don't you look into counselling services? They must have some sort of job where you could use your training but do something that would appeal to you more.

Grace: You're right. There's no sense in just **griping** about it. I'll see if I can find out about other jobs. I could take a couple of evening courses for more training. I just don't want to do a whole different program.

Hillary: I'm sure **there's** lots of jobs you'd be good at.

Grace: And maybe they'd even pay more! Or is that asking too much?

Discussion

1. Why does Grace want to change jobs? Describe her feelings.
2. In your own words, describe Hillary's boss and Grace's boss.
3. In pairs, develop and role play a dialogue in which one student gives the other advice on looking for a job or changing careers.

THE JOB INTERVIEW

Harris: Miss Joanne Winters? Please come in and sit down. Make yourself comfortable.

Winters: Thank you, Mr. Harris.

Harris: Now, Miss Winters, may I ask why you are interested in this particular job?

Winters: Well, I've always enjoyed working with people and I **have a good head** for mathematics and statistics. When I saw the opportunity your company was offering, I **jumped at** it.

Harris: I notice from your application that you have no experience in doing opinion polls.

Winters: That's true; however, I do have related experience. I've taken journalism courses and worked for the campus newspaper, so I've done several interviews. I also worked one summer in a tourist information office and I'm quite comfortable talking with the public.

Harris: I see that you're working for Bradshaw Industries right now. Why do you wish to leave that position?

Winters: Right now I'm only working part-time there and with the present situation they may be **laying off** office employees. And, frankly, I would rather have a job dealing with the public; **typing and filing** all day **is** really not challenging enough for me.

Harris: So I may contact your current employer as a **reference**?

Winters: Yes, certainly.

Harris: Fine. Why do you think you are the person for our company, Miss Winters?

Winters: Well—I believe I can be an asset to Canada Wide Surveys. This job interests me very much and I know that I can do it well. Your company has an excellent reputation for a **top-notch** staff and I'm sure I wouldn't disappoint you.

Harris: Thank you. I understand you have all the **particulars** concerning the position. Do you have any questions?

Winters: No, I don't think so.

Harris: Well, we do have many applicants still to see. We should be able to let you know one way or the other sometime next week. Thank you for coming.

Winters: Thank you for taking the time to see me, Mr. Harris. Good-bye.

to have a head for—(idiomatic) to be good at or talented in (usually used with mathematics or arithmetic)

jump at—(colloquial) to seize an opportunity eagerly

lay off—to put out of work temporarily, to discharge

typing and filing ... is—a singular verb with a plural subject is often heard in speech, but is considered incorrect in formal English

reference—person asked about one's character or ability

top-notch—(colloquial) excellent, first-rate

particulars—details, information

Discussion

1. Is this dialogue formal or informal? What are some of the expressions that reveal this?

2. Do you think Joanne Winters will get the job? Why or why not?

3. Role play a job interview for the class. In a class discussion, evaluate each interview. Should the candidate get the job? Why or why not?

4. In small groups, go through "Help Wanted" ads and pick out a few interesting positions. Discuss the qualifications and personal characteristics that would be necessary for the job.

LANGUAGE NOTES

Formal and Informal English

Different registers (levels) of a language are required in different situations. Informal English is used in many everyday conversations and in friendly letters. Formal English is required in most writing and in more formal speaking situations. Job interviews, speeches, many business dealings, and conversations with people of authority, such as employers, require formal English.

Formal spoken English is closer to written English in form and style. Sentences can be long and complex; words and pronunciation are precise. Informal English, on the other hand, is characterized by the use of colloquialisms, slang, and short forms. Sounds are often reduced and references are less precise; words such as "stuff" and "thingamajig" are used, for example.

Compare these examples of some of the differences:

Informal	Formal
Yeah	Yes
I dunno	I don't know
pretty bad	quite bad
a lot of	many
this aft	this afternoon

Change the informal English into more formal English in the following dialogue.

Interviewer: Good morning, Mr. O'Connor. How are you today?

Sean: Pretty good, I guess. How 'bout you?

Interviewer: Fine, thank you. The interview should only take half an hour. First of all, we'd like you to write a short essay.

Sean: Yeah, sure. What about?

Interviewer: We'd like you to explain your views on the use of computers in this business.

Sean: You know, I don't know a lot about your business, but I'll give it a go, okay? Anyway, when it comes to computers—that's my thing. I know a lot about them.

Interviewer: Please take a seat here—I'll return in 15 minutes.

Sean: You bet.

Subject-Verb Agreement

A compound subject joined by *and* requires a plural verb unless the parts of the subject are thought of as one unit, as in the following examples:

Bread and butter is something I should avoid on my diet.
Is the salt and pepper on the table?

In informal spoken English, *there's*, *here's*, and *where's* are often used with plural predicates. This use is actually ungrammatical and not acceptable in formal or written English. In speech, however, it is easier to pronounce *there's* than *there are* or *there're*.

There's a lot of novels on that shelf.
Where's my boots?
Here's the papers you wanted.

Talent Idioms

There are a number of idioms that describe different talents. Many of these refer to parts of the body:

She has a head for figures.
I have no ear for music.
An interior designer must have a good eye for colour.
A good reporter has a nose for news.
He's very good with plants; he has a green thumb.
She never gives away what she is thinking—she has a real poker face.
A good lecturer must have the gift of the gab.
He has a silver tongue—he can talk anyone into anything.

Similar idioms are used for a lack of talent:

I can't dance—I have two left feet.
He's so clumsy—all thumbs at everything he tries.
I'm not very good at music—I have a tin ear.

CULTURE NOTE

Canadians feel that what they do for a living is extremely important. A job often determines social standing in the community, and the amount of money earned often defines lifestyle.

Besides earning a living and having social standing, Canadians generally want to get ahead and be successful in their chosen fields. Such is the "work ethic" prevalent in Canadian society. This traditional attitude fostered by the first immigrants in Canada still holds for many people. They believe if they work hard, they can find success for themselves and their families.

Still, there have been many changes in the workplace in recent years. Traditionally, sons followed in their fathers' footsteps when choosing an occupation, and daughters became housewives and mothers. But today, Canadians have many career choices available to them and many change careers often in a lifetime. A job may become obsolete because of changing technology, for example, and a person then has to be retrained. In our changing society no job is secure.

Women's roles in the workplace have changed dramatically in the past ten years. Women are now choosing careers rather than holding temporary jobs forced upon them by poor economic conditions. In the past, many husbands felt embarrassed or threatened if their wives worked outside the home. That is not the case today. As social and economic conditions change, Canadian women are vigorously pursuing careers.

Thus the work ethic is a large part of Canadian life. Men and women generally work hard to achieve success and satisfaction. Often the reward is wealth and material possessions. Sometimes, however, people become workaholics, driving themselves so hard that they suffer emotional and health problems. Fortunately, most Canadians have learned to balance both work and leisure time through hobbies and socializing. In short, Canadians do believe they can "work hard and play hard."

Additional Vocabulary

trade—skilled, mechanical work (e.g., machine technician)

profession—occupation requiring special education and training (e.g., medicine or law)

salary—fixed annual rate of pay usually for professional and office work (e.g., a salary of $20 000)

wage—fixed hourly rate of pay usually for manual and physical work (e.g., a wage of $5.60 an hour)

résumé—brief account of one's career, qualifications, and employment history

curriculum vitae (C.V.)—(Latin) résumé for academic purposes, dealing extensively with education

Discussion Topics

1. If you could choose any occupation, which would you choose and why?
2. Do you believe "One works to live" or "One lives to work"? Explain the difference.
3. What advice would you give someone looking for a job?
4. Which occupations do you feel are the most stressful?
5. What are the pros and cons of working full-time and raising a family? For both parents? For one parent alone?
6. Which jobs do you feel have the most status in our society?
7. What are the health risks of being a workaholic?
8. Discuss how a financial value is placed on work. Does higher education always mean a higher income? What do you think should determine a salary? List possible criteria.
9. Sexism is a controversial issue in the workforce. Do you think men and women should get equal pay for equal work?

Activities

1. In pairs, develop and role play a dialogue of an employment counsellor discussing different job opportunities with a client.
2. In pairs, develop and role play a dialogue in which a boss fires an employee.

Assignments

1. Visit a Canada Employment Centre and find out what jobs are available. Look through any available information giving advice to job-seekers.
2. Research information on how to write a job application letter and a résumé.
3. Look at various job application forms and compare the questions that are asked.

four
Leisure Time

MYSTERY BUFFS

pretty quiet—(colloquial) fairly quiet

Agatha Christie whodunit—murder mystery by Agatha Christie; whodunit is from "who done (non-standard for "did") it?": "it" refers to the murder

all-star cast—cast of famous actors and actresses

eccentric—odd, unusual

figure out—solve the mystery or problem

hunch—intuitive feeling, suspicion

catch on—understand, see the significance of

you—(colloquial) people in general

play along—join the game

the butler did it—an old cliche of murder mysteries; butler is the chief male servant of a household

spill the beans—(colloquial) reveal a secret

salt mine—(colloquial) work

Richard:	How was your weekend?
Carolyn:	**Pretty quiet**. Just did a few things around the house. I spent Saturday night curled up in front of the fire with a book. Did you do anything interesting?
Richard:	Jackie and I went to see the new movie at the Capitol.
Carolyn:	Oh, yeah? Any good?
Richard:	Not bad. It's an **Agatha Christie whodunit**.
Carolyn:	Oh, I like those. An **all-star cast**, I suppose.
Richard:	Yeah, all playing **eccentric** characters—the type you only see in murder mysteries.
Carolyn:	Did you **figure out** who the murderer was?
Richard:	I had a **hunch** but I didn't **catch on** to all the clues.
Carolyn:	Did the detective call all the suspects together at the end?
Richard:	Yeah, and he went over the clues and the possible motives, and just when it looked like they all could have done it, he revealed the murderer's identity.
Carolyn:	Well, don't tell me who did it. I want to see that movie and it's no fun if **you** can't **play along**.
Richard:	Okay, I won't tell you that the **butler did it**.
Carolyn:	Richard!
Richard:	Just kidding. There wasn't even a butler in the film.
Carolyn:	Well, maybe I'd better get going before you really do **spill the beans**. Back to the old **salt mine**.
Richard:	I should get back to work myself. Bye.
Carolyn:	See you later.

Discussion

1. Where do you think this dialogue is taking place?
2. Who do you think Jackie is?
3. How does Richard tease Carolyn?
4. Develop and role play a dialogue starting with the question: "What did you do on the weekend?"
5. Do you read mystery novels or watch detective shows? Do you get involved in solving the mysteries?

WEEKEND HOBBIES

Chris: Thank goodness it's Friday. I've been looking forward to the weekend since Monday.

Anne: I thought you enjoyed your work.

Chris: Oh, I do. I mean, it's not that bad. But I'm not a **workaholic** or anything. I really appreciate my time off.

Anne: I don't like weekends—all those chores to do around the house.

Chris: I try to do most of that on weeknights and leave the weekend free.

Anne: To do what?

Chris: Oh, different things. Right now **I'm really into** painting. I spend my Sundays in the country doing **landscapes**.

Anne: I didn't know you were an artist.

Chris: Calling my painting art is really **stretching it**. I just like to **dabble** in it. And I also do some racquet sports on the weekends—squash and tennis.

Anne: How do you find time for all of that?

Chris: Just takes a bit of organization. My leisure time is important to me— so I make time. And look at Greg—you know those **ceramic** pieces he's always making at home? Well, he sells them to a local **handicrafts** store. Fun *and* profit.

Anne: I'm afraid I'm **all thumbs** when it comes to things like that.

Chris: Do you have any hobbies?

Anne: Nothing I **stick to**. I used to play guitar when I was a kid. Last year I thought of **taking up** photography but the equipment can be so expensive.

Chris: But you could get into it gradually. No need to **go overboard** with fancy equipment. You've got a good camera already and if you take a course at the community centre you'll have access to their darkroom facilities once in a while.

Anne: I've always been something of a **shutterbug**. It would be nice to learn more about it.

Chris: And it could be useful—for gifts.

Anne: That's true—maybe I should look into it again.

workaholic—(colloquial) non-stop worker, someone addicted to working

I'm really into—(slang) I'm extremely interested in

landscapes—drawings and paintings of outdoor scenes

stretching it—(colloquial) exaggerating

dabble—play, do something for fun; not seriously

ceramic—pottery, made of clay

handicrafts—any art using the hands (e.g., pottery, weaving)

all thumbs—(idiomatic) clumsy

stick to—keep doing

take up—begin, start

go overboard—go too far, be over-enthusiastic

shutterbug—(colloquial) someone who likes taking pictures

Discussion

1. Where and when is this dialogue taking place?
2. Name and describe the leisure time activities mentioned in the dialogue.
3. What are the characteristics of a workaholic?
4. What leisure time activities do you enjoy most?
5. What new hobbies or activities would you like to take up?

LANGUAGE NOTES

Noun Compounds

In English, nouns often function as adjectives to describe other nouns. The first noun, or the noun/adjective, specifically explains and describes the second noun, categorizing it:

>   a stamp collector
>   an Agatha Christie mystery
>   a racquetball player

Other adjectives come before the noun/adjective:

>   an interesting detective story
>   the white-haired antique collector

Noun compounds are formed through the use of nouns as adjectives. Some noun compounds are written as two words, some are hyphenated, and others become one word:

cassette tape	bottle-opener	bookcase
tennis court	stamp-collector	housework
bus station	baby-food	raincoat

Make the following phrases into noun compounds where possible:

1. a machine for videos
2. a cup of water
3. tickets for the theatre
4. a bar of soap
5. a magazine for travel

Make the following noun compounds into noun phrases:

1. a bird house
2. a glass coffee table
3. a picture frame
4. a fountain pen
5. a coffee cup

Declarative Intonation

Declarative, or rising-falling, intonation is used for statements, clauses, and for "wh" questions (those using the interrogatives *who*, *what*, etc.). These all end with a downward glide of the voice on the last accented syllable. The fall of the voice indicates to the listener that the speaker has finished the statement. (A speaker stays on a middle pitch if he or she pauses before the end of the statement.) From a normal tone, the voice rises on the stressed syllable and then falls.

Practise this intonation pattern in the following sentences:

1. I had a few things to do around the house.
2. It's a black and white movie.
3. I love water colours.
4. There's a horror movie playing downtown.
5. This is the latest bestseller.
6. Science fiction is very popular among teen-agers.
7. Squash is always a good work-out.
8. On weekends I like to putter around the garden.
9. All the shows seem to be about doctors, detectives, and lawyers.
10. That play had a pretty thin plot.

Qualifiers

In informal spoken English, there are a number of qualifiers which are used with adjectives. Some of these (such as *pretty* and *real*) are not used in formal English. The varying strength of these qualifiers can often be confusing.

a little, a little bit	weakest
kind of, sort of	
pretty, quite, rather	
real, really, terribly, awfully	strongest

Quite and *rather* are more common in British English. *Real* in front of an adjective is considered very informal, even slang. *Pretty* is used frequently in speech.

Examples:

1. I'm kind of tired—maybe I should stay home tonight.
2. He's really glad to be going home; he hated it here.
3. It's quite far—maybe you should take a bus.
4. No, he won't be seeing a doctor; he's just a little under the weather.
5. I was awfully scared when I heard the siren so close.

Complete each dialogue with a qualifier.

1. *A.* How was your weekend?
   B. Horrible! I'm _____ exhausted. I was busy all weekend.
2. *A.* What did you think of the play?
   B. I thought it was _____ boring actually.
3. *A.* That magazine article was _____ insulting.

B. No kidding! It used every name-calling technique you could think of.
4. *A.* Chess is hard to learn, isn't it?
   B. _____. Actually, it's _____ easy to learn, _____ difficult to master.
5. *A.* It was _____ cold out at the campsite.
   B. That's for sure. I had to wear two sweaters and stay by the campfire.

CULTURE NOTE

Television has become an integral part of North American culture. Not only is it a popular way to spend leisure time, but it also transmits and reflects aspects of culture.

North American television is very commercially oriented. Many people from other countries find the commercials on TV annoying. But North Americans are used to the constant barrage, and many learn to tune it out. Some use commercials as a break-time from television, but they are not immune to the effects of commercials. Many viewers know commercial jingles and slogans by heart.

The quality of commercials varies considerably. Some are extremely annoying and insulting; advertisers feel that these are nevertheless effective. Making an impression, being memorable, sells products. Consumers often complain about the content of commercials, however, and some advertisers do listen. The portrayal of women as either house-

wives or sex objects has come under fire and advertisers are slowly moving away from these images. Children's toy commercials are also criticized for their hard-hitting sales techniques. Most Canadians recognize that advertisers are supporting the television industry and that commercials are the price we have to pay.

Canadian television is dominated by programs originating in the United States. Although the CRTC (Canadian Radio-Television and Telecommunications Commission) demands Canadian content on the airwaves, most Canadians can receive a number of American channels. Many feel that the overwhelming influence of American television in Canada is not beneficial and that it makes our country seem more American than it is. For example, Canadians who watch American police and detective programs tend to have a better understanding and knowledge of American laws than Canadian laws. This can lead to

problems when they wrongly assume that the Canadian legal system works in the same way as the American system.

Sex and violence on television is another debated issue. Many people feel that violence on TV encourages people to commit crimes in real life. While there are controls on how sexually explicit television programs can be, services such as Pay-TV and specialty channels available to those with satellite television do have adult-oriented programming. While some feel that there should be no censorship in a democratic society, others feel that there is a dangerous link between sex and violence on television and in real life, and that, as a result, such programs should be censored.

Still, an extremely wide variety of programming is available on television today. Television can be an important educational tool, as well as a source of entertainment. Canadian television has some of the world's best documentaries and public affairs programs. Cable services often carry local channels which broadcast university lectures and school plays. Correspondence courses with televised lectures are also available. Although Canadians complain about North American television, there is enough choice to please almost everyone—programs include religious shows, sports events, adventures, and children's shows.

Additional Vocabulary

censor—edit or repress material, such as passages in a book or scenes in a movie, for political or moral reasons

dub—to change the sound track, especially the voices, of a movie (e.g., foreign films playing in Canada sometimes have English-speaking actors speaking the parts)

sub-titles—translated text of a film appearing in print at the bottom of the screen

different genres of movies and books:
    mystery, thriller, suspense, detective story
    horror
    science fiction, fantasy
    romance
    comedy, humour
    western
    historical fiction
    non-fiction, documentary
    biography

pastimes and hobbies:
    card games (bridge, poker, gin, euchre, cribbage)
    board games (chess, checkers, Monopoly, Scrabble)
    trivia games
    puzzles (jigsaws, crosswords)
    collecting (coins, stamps, knick-knacks, souvenirs)
    crafts (sewing, quilting, crocheting, woodwork, ceramics)
    dancing (ballroom, disco, folk)
    video games

sports:
    fishing, hunting, camping
    cycling, hiking, jogging, swimming
    canoeing, sailing, surfing, skiing, skating
    badminton, tennis, racquetball, squash, ping-pong
    volleyball, basketball, football, soccer, baseball
    hockey, lacrosse, golf, pool
    martial arts (judo, karate)
    gymnastics
    weight-lifting, track, aerobics

music:
    listening (rock, country 'n western, folk, jazz, classical, opera)
    playing instruments (piano, guitar, flute, violin, drums)

reading:
    paperbacks, hardcovers, novels, bestsellers

places to visit:
    museums, galleries, theatres, movies
    zoo, aquarium, circus
    sports stadium and arena
    amusement parks, exhibitions

Discussion Topics

1. What do you like and/or dislike about North American television?
2. What is your favourite and least favourite commercial? Do you think it is effective? Why?
3. Do you think there should be less sex and violence on television?
4. What books or movies do you enjoy? Why?
5. What kind of music do you enjoy listening to?
6. What are your favourite sports? Do you watch or participate? Do you prefer team or individual sports?
7. If you could start a collection, what would you collect?
8. What genre of art do you like? Do you like modern art?
9. Do you think Canadians have too much or too little leisure time? Do they spend their leisure time wisely?
10. What do you find different about leisure time in Canada and in your country?

Activities

1. Organize some leisure-time activities. Bring board games and card games to class. In small groups, try to learn new games. Play charades or other party games.
2. Watch a segment of a TV show in class. Analyze it in terms of frequency and quality of commercials, American vs. Canadian content, and the presence of violence.
3. In small groups, act out commercials or scenes from favourite movies or TV shows.

4. Have a classroom debate on one of the following topics:
   (a) Television, movies, and books should be more strictly censored.
   (b) Our work week should be reduced and our leisure time increased.
   (c) Television is a negative influence on society.

Assignments

1. Prepare a short oral report on your favourite movie, TV show, book, or game and present it to the class.

2. Make a list of movies playing in your town or city and classify them according to type (science fiction, comedy, etc.).
3. Make a summary of the rules of a sport or game.
4. Research one other leisure-time activity that may interest you and describe it to the class.
5. Expand on the list of leisure-time activities given in this unit.

five
Food for Thought

DINING OUT

Jane: Let's go out for dinner tonight. I forgot to take something out of the freezer and **it's been ages** since we've been out.

Mike: Good idea. Where do you feel like going?

Jane: Oh, **I dunno**. How about the Golden Dragon?

Mike: No, let's forget about being health conscious today. I'm in the mood for something heavier than **stir-fried** meat and vegetables. There's a new Italian place somebody at work was **raving about**.

Jane: No, all that pasta and those **rich sauces** are too **heavy** for me—too many calories. Let's look in the Dining Guide in the newspaper . . . Hmmm, this Japanese place has good reviews.

Mike: Nah, that raw fish we had last time wasn't bad, but . . .

Jane: This place is different. They cut up the food and cook it in front of you. It's supposed to be quite a show.

Mike: How about steak or roast beef?

Jane: They're easy enough to cook at home. Seafood?

Mike: Too fishy. Mexican food?

Jane: That spicy food always gives me heartburn. Maybe some good onion soup?

Mike: Or pizza?

Jane: No, too close to **junk food**.

Mike: How about that German place on Main Street? A good, hearty meat and potatoes dinner.

Jane: Here's something that sounds interesting—"The Great Canadian **Smorgasbord**"—they say they have something for everyone.

Mike: Great, let's go.

it's been ages—it's been a long time

I dunno—reduced form of "I don't know"

stir-fried—fried quickly over high heat with constant stirring; method used in Oriental cooking

to rave about—to speak enthusiastically about

rich sauces—sauces made with a lot of butter and cream

heavy—hard to digest, rich

junk food—food with little nutritional value, particularly potato chips, soft drinks, candy

smorgasbord (or **smorg**)—(Swedish word) buffet offering a wide variety of dishes, hot and cold

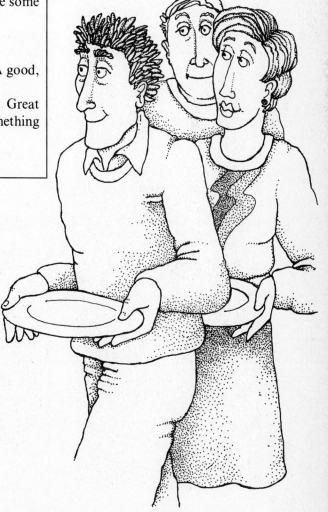

Discussion

1. How would you characterize Jane's food tastes? And Mike's?

2. What foods do you think will be served at the smorgasbord? What foods would you consider typically Canadian?

3. What stereotypical characteristics of various ethnic cuisines are mentioned? Are these descriptions accurate?

4. Is the ethnic food served in restaurants always authentic? Are the dishes the same as those served in homes?

5. Canadians eat out often. Why do you think this is so?

6. Do you like to eat out? What kinds of restaurants do you like?

THE DINNER PARTY

worrywart—(colloquial) someone who worries too much

picky—(colloquial) too fussy or particular

beef stroganoff—dish of cut-up beef with mushrooms and sour cream

flop—(colloquial) failure

get to you—(slang) bother you

tried and true—well-tested

trifle—British dessert made with cake, whipped cream, custard, fruit, and sherry

from scratch—from basic ingredients, not from a mix

gotcha—spoken reduction of "I've got you," meaning "Okay" or "I understand"

Doug:	I guess we'd better get our shopping list together for the dinner party.
Beth:	(sighs) I suppose so. I've been trying not to think about it.
Doug:	Oh, don't be such a **worrywart**. Everything will turn out all right.
Beth:	But my sister is so **picky**. And so many things could go wrong. Remember that **beef stroganoff**? It was a **flop**! Charlene still talks about it.
Doug:	Don't let her **get to you**. It was just one little mistake. And this time we're using all our **tried and true** recipes . . . (writing a list) Let's see—we need some veal, mushrooms, salad, vegetables . . .
Beth:	. . . cheese, crackers, asparagus.
Doug:	What are we serving for an appetizer?
Beth:	How about if you make your famous shrimp dip with crackers and raw vegetables?
Doug:	Okay. And dessert?
Beth:	**Trifle**?
Doug:	Mmmm, sounds good. Do you want me to pick up a sponge cake?
Beth:	No, I'll make the cake **from scratch**. Charlene always claims she can tell the difference.
Doug:	Need anything for the cake?
Beth:	No, I stocked up on some staples last week—including baking supplies. You could pick up some sherry, though.
Doug:	**Gotcha**. I can pick all this up Friday night after work and then Saturday won't be so rushed.
Beth:	Let's just hope my sister arrives in a good mood!

Discussion

1. Why is Beth worried?
2. What could have happened to the beef stroganoff?
3. Which food preparations will be Beth's responsibility and which will be Doug's?
4. Have you ever been in a similar situation? Did you ever have to give a special dinner party which you were worried about? Did everything go well?
5. Do you like to cook? What dishes do you cook?
6. In small groups, plan menus for different occasions. For example, plan:

   (a) a lunch for a few co-workers
   (b) a dinner for your employer
   (c) the first dinner for your future in-laws

LANGUAGE NOTES

Question Intonation

A rising intonation is used at the end of Yes/No questions. There is an upward glide of the voice on the last accented syllable. It is especially important to remember this intonation for sentences and sentence fragments which are meant as questions, but are not in the inverted form. The rising intonation should be used in the following examples taken from the dialogues:

> Seafood?
> Mexican food?
> And dessert?
> Trifle?

Practise the rising intonation in the following questions:

1. Could I have a salad instead of french fries with my hamburger?
2. Do you want your steak rare or medium?
3. Is the cake home-made?
4. Is coffee included with the breakfast special?
5. Is the wine list extensive?
6. Would you like the salad bar with that?
7. Do you take any charge cards?
8. Would you like an after-dinner drink?
9. The restaurant's far from here?
10. Coffee or tea?

Expressions with *In* and *Out*

There are a number of idiomatic expressions with *in* and *out* in informal English:

I like to *eat out* once in a while—somebody to serve me and no dishes to wash. (eat in a restaurant)

To know how to package the food, the attendant at the fast-food counter asks: "Will that be *to eat in or take out?*" (to eat inside the restaurant or to take the food out)

James and Cindy have been *going out* for a long time now. (dating)

Is Mr. Thomas *in*? (in the office)
No, I'm sorry. He just *went out* a few minutes ago. (left)

Fred *knows all the ins and outs of* the insurance business. (is fully experienced in, knows all about)

They say that short skirts will be *in* once again this year, and that the baggy look is definitely *out*. (in fashion, in style) (out of fashion)

Don't tell me the postal workers are *out* again! (out on strike)

I'd better call you. I'll be *in and out* of the office all day.

Why don't you *go out* for a change and have some fun? No, I'd better *stay in* and do some work.

CULTURE NOTE

Canadians often entertain by inviting people to dinner. It is customary to arrive on time for a dinner party and to bring a bottle of wine or a small impersonal gift, such as flowers or candy. Food is not brought unless specifically asked for by the hosts, as, for example, at a potluck dinner, where everyone contributes a food item.

Some meals may include appetizers, soup, or salad before the main course. A typical main course includes meat or fish, potatoes or rice, and one or two vegetables. Dessert is usually served with coffee or tea at the end of the meal. Sometimes a dinner is served as a buffet; people then serve themselves from a table that is set with a variety of foods.

Table manners can vary from culture to culture. Even the way utensils are handled can be different. In Europe, diners tend to keep their

forks in the left hand throughout a meal; in North America, the fork is often switched to the right hand after food is cut.

Canadians tend to eat a large meal anywhere from five to nine o'clock in the evening. Some families will say grace (a prayer of thanks) before a meal. It is polite to finish all the food on a plate, if possible. An empty or near empty wine glass will be continually refilled by the hosts. Canadians also consider it impolite to make noise while eating and drinking.

To show that you enjoyed a meal, it is polite to compliment the quality of the food. Be sure to accept a second helping if you like the food and are not full; Canadian hosts will usually offer it only once and will take a refusal at face value. In some other cultures, however, it is polite to refuse up to three times before accepting a second helping.

Eating out is also popular in Canada. Canadians enjoy a wide variety of cuisines. There are many different eating places—cafeterias, fast-food outlets, and formal restaurants. At restaurants with table service, tipping the waiter or waitress is customary.

Food likes and dislikes vary from culture to culture and can be a source of intense personal prejudice. What is disgusting to one person can be a delicacy to another. Canadians are generally conservative in their food tastes but, because of the number of different ethnic groups in Canada, they have also learned to appreciate many different kinds of cuisine. A Canadian family may enjoy Italian food one night, Chinese food the next—then Greek or Ukrainian. The ability to enjoy many different kinds of foods is highly regarded in Canada. Exploring the cuisine of different cultures is not only fun, but also a good learning experience.

Additional Vocabulary

brunch—combination of breakfast and lunch, served late in the morning or early afternoon, usually on Sunday

fast-food—hamburgers, special sandwiches and such, served quickly for eat in or take out

drive-in—restaurant where you order through an intercom, food is brought on a tray, and you eat in your car

drive-through—take-out system; you order through an intercom, pick up food at the window, and take it home without leaving your car

licensed restaurant—restaurant that has a liquor licence to serve beer, wine, and other alcoholic beverages

caterer—business that prepares food for parties and banquets in a home or rented premises

cafeteria—informal restaurant, especially in schools and office buildings, where customers select food from a counter and take it to the tables themselves

barbecue—several uses are common: outdoor grill; meat cooked on a grill; spicy tomato sauce used on the food; party or picnic where barbecued foods are served

cuisine—(Fr.) style of cooking

gourmet—(Fr.) someone who enjoys and is an excellent judge of high quality food and drink

Discussion Topics

1. Describe some Canadian eating customs that are different from those in your culture.
2. Describe your favourite meal.
3. Do you like to shop for food? What do you think of the price and availability of food in Canada? How do you shop for bargains?
4. Discuss the changing roles of men and women with regard to the preparation and serving of food.

Activities

1. Look at a few sample menus and discuss the foods available and their price. Practise placing orders from the menus.
2. In small groups, look at different cookbooks to see how recipes are written. Discuss the different foods. Try out a simple recipe in class.
3. Have a potluck supper including various ethnic foods.

Assignments

1. Make a list of the different kinds of ethnic restaurants in your city or region.
2. Make a shopping list for a special meal and consult the food store ads in the newspaper to find the best prices for the foods on your list.
3. Locate an interesting recipe in the food section of your newspaper. Identify common cooking terms.
4. Look through a Canadian cookbook. Identify the kinds of foods that are common in different Canadian provinces. What dishes are common in Québec for example?
5. Read the restaurant reviews in a newspaper or magazine. Prepare your own review of a restaurant you have tried and present it to the class.

six

Survival of the Fittest

his stretching

sneakers

leotards

THE FITNESS CRAZE

Janice:	So when are we going to get together to finish off this report?
Debbie:	Well, I'm free most of the week. Tuesdays and Thursdays I have my fitness class, though. ~~(though.)~~ *except*
Janice:	Fitness class! How do you find the energy? After a day in here, I'm too **bushed** for anything but supper and TV.
Debbie:	But I find that getting a good **work-out** a couple times a week actually makes me feel more energetic. You should try it.
Janice:	What kind of class is it?
Debbie:	**Aerobics**—it's fun, a lot of dance-type steps.
Janice:	Dance? I've got **two left feet**—I can't dance.
Stuart:	(joining the conversation) Don't worry about it, Jan. I'm no **Fred Astaire** myself. When I first started aerobics I felt pretty **self-conscious**, but everybody's too busy **huffing and puffing** to notice anyone else.
Janice:	*You* take aerobics, too! What is this—an **epidemic**?
Debbie:	Sure, haven't you heard? Everyone's getting into the fitness **craze**—especially us **baby boomers**— **Participaction** and **all that jazz**. Why don't you come and try out my class? They have a drop-in fee if you're not a regular.
Janice:	I don't know about this. Where is this class anyway?
Debbie:	It's at the community centre near my place.
Janice:	Is that where you go too, Stu?
Stuart:	No, the **Y** down the street—I go on my lunch hour.
Janice:	Where will I get the gym **leotards**, though?
Debbie:	I just wear a T-shirt and sweat pants. And you need to have a good pair of runners. How about coming to my place after work tomorrow? We can go to the class and then work on the report afterwards.
Janice:	I suppose I might as well **jump on the bandwagon**, as they say. But it'll probably kill me.
Stuart:	**No sweat.** Just take it easy the first night.

bushed—(slang) tired, exhausted

work-out—intense exercise session

aerobics—exercises designed to increase heart action, usually dance-type exercises done to music

have two left feet—(idiomatic) be clumsy, unable to dance

Fred Astaire—well-known American dancer

self-conscious—uncomfortably aware of one's own appearance and actions, embarrassed in front of other people

huffing and puffing—(colloquial) breathing hard

epidemic—widespread occurrence; usually used for diseases

craze—fad, strong interest

baby boomers—the large number of people born during the baby boom (1946-1962)

Participaction—term coined by the Canadian government in the 1970s to promote fitness

all that jazz—(slang) and everything else

Y—short for YMCA (Young Men's Christian Association) or YWCA (Young Women's Christian Association), organizations which run residences, social programs, and various community activities

leotards—tight-fitting dance and exercise clothes

jump on the bandwagon—(idiomatic) join in on what everyone else is doing

no sweat—(slang) no problem

Discussion

1. Where could this conversation be taking place?
2. Can you find the pun (play on words) in this dialogue?
3. What is your favourite way to keep fit? Why do you enjoy it?
4. Change the dialogue so that Debbie is trying to persuade Janice to go jogging or swimming. Practise dialogue variations in pairs.
5. Some companies now offer fitness breaks instead of coffee breaks and have gym facilities at the workplace. What do you think of this trend? Can you think of similar ways to make fitness activities more accessible?

sir♂ = ma'am♀   *father   mother*
dad   mum   Mom

HEALTH FOOD!?

hon—short for "honey"; a term of endearment

rabbit food—(slang, derogatory) salad, green vegetables

c'mon—reduced form of "come on"; interjection meaning "You must be kidding"

fibre—indigestible part of plants and grains which aids digestion

do away with—(colloquial) get rid of, abolish, destroy, kill

to have a sweet tooth—(idiomatic) to be fond of sweets and desserts

low-cal—low in calories, nonfattening

nagged into—continually complained and reminded until a habit is changed

easy on the salt—use the salt sparingly

Liz: Supper's ready, **hon**.

Gary: Okay, I'm coming . . . Hey, what's this? A salad for supper?

Liz: Well, it's too hot to cook. And anyway, it's good for you. The doctor said you should eat more greens.

Gary: How do you expect me to survive on **rabbit food**?

Liz: **C'mon**, it's not so bad. There's tuna in there for protein, as well as the lettuce and vegetables.

Gary: All right, all right . . . Where's the white bread?

Liz: I didn't buy any. Here's some whole wheat rolls—more **fibre**, you know.

Gary: Did you **do away with** dessert too?

Liz: Well, I know what a **sweet tooth** you have, so I made a fruit dessert. You'll never know it's **low-cal**.

Gary: Last year you **nagged me into** quitting smoking and now you're trying to reform my eating habits—when will it all end?

Liz: When you're perfect. Besides, I only do it because I care about you . . . Oh, and **easy on the salt**.

Discussion

1. Where do you think this dialogue is taking place? What is the relationship between Liz and Gary?

2. Describe how Liz is trying to improve Gary's health. What do you think of the health food craze?

3. In small groups, make a list of foods which are considered healthy and those which are not. Decide on five tips for eating well. Compare your list with that of other groups and discuss any differences.

LANGUAGE NOTES

Nicknames and Terms of Address

Many names in English have shortened forms that are used as nicknames. Some people do not like nicknames, however, and others may prefer one particular nickname over others. It is best to find out about personal preferences before using a nickname.

Examples of nicknames:

> Alexander—Al, Alex, Sandy
> Barbara—Barb, Barbie, Babs
> Charles—Charlie, Chuck
> Deborah—Debbie, Deb
> Edward—Ed, Eddie, Ted, Ned
> Elizabeth—Liz, Eliza, Beth, Bess, Lizzie, Elly, Betty
> Katherine—Kathy, Kate, Kit, Kitty, Katie, Kay
> Margaret—Marge, Meg, Margie, Peggy, Margo, Greta, Rita
> Robert—Bob, Rob, Bobby, Robbie
> William—Will, Bill, Willie, Billy

Nicknames ending in *-y* or *-ie* are often used for children.

Some nicknames are not shortened forms of given names. For example, "Chip" is sometimes used as a nickname for a boy who has the same name as his father (e.g., William Mark Laughton, Jr.). Other nicknames are based on physical characteristics or personality traits. A red-haired person may sometimes be called "Red" and a tall person may have the nickname "Stretch."

Other forms of endearment may be used between a husband and wife or a boyfriend and girlfriend. In English, common endearments include: honey, sweetheart, darling, sugar, dear. Other forms of address, often used to get someone's attention, include: buddy, mac, hey you, dearie. These terms, however, are very informal and may be considered offensive. Although you may hear them, they should be avoided.

A helpful rule to remember is that the form of the name given in an introduction usually reflects an individual's preference.

Giving Advice

Giving advice is always difficult to do tactfully. Many people resent getting advice, and even when they ask for it, they may be simply seeking approval.

The modal or auxiliary verbs *should* and *ought to* are commonly used to give advice; however, they are quite strong when used without qualifying phrases:

> You should quit smoking.
> You ought to get that transmission checked.

An opening phrase and a tentative tone of voice can make such suggestions more polite:

> I think you should . . .
> It seems to me that you could . . .

Modal verbs such as *might* and *may* can further soften a suggestion:

> Joining an exercise class might be a good idea.

Using a rising intonation makes a suggestion more like a question:

> Perhaps you might want to look for a new job?

Clarifying the pros and cons of a problem is also a tactful way of giving advice:

> One advantage of a holiday is that you'll have time to relax; at the same time, it might be too costly right now.

On the other hand, to make a suggestion more forceful, the speaker may begin with a phrase that indicates conviction:

> I believe this would be the better road to take.

The most forceful way to state an opinion or give advice is to express it bluntly without qualifiers:

> This is a serious problem and you must do something about it immediately.

The tone of voice accompanying any suggestion or advice is very important. For instance, tentative suggestions require an encouraging and mild tone. On the other hand, a strong opinion or conviction requires a more forceful and firmer tone.

Place the appropriate modal auxiliary in the following sentences according to the kind of advice that is being offered.

1. You really _____ get your hair cut! It looks so long and shaggy.
2. I thought that you _____ want to consider several different kinds of diets before choosing one.
3. His hacking and coughing are really getting out of hand; he _____ quit smoking!
4. If you don't want to eat Italian food tonight, you _____ prefer going out to a French restaurant.
5. On the one hand, you have quite a bit of money saved; on the other hand, you _____ blow it all on a spa membership!

Stress Differences

Several pairs of words in English are distinguished in pronunciation by a difference in stress. *Dessert* and *desert*, for example, are two words which are often confused. There is a difference in stress, as well as in spelling and meaning.

A désert is an area of very hot, dry land. A dessért is a sweet food served at the end of a meal.

The following are examples of words which have a first-syllable stress if they are nouns, a second-syllable stress if they are verbs:

conflict	decrease	present
contest	increase	progress
contrast	object	subject

Practise the following sentences. Pay close attention to the marked accented syllables.

1. I'll condúct you to your room.
2. I'm concerned about your cónduct.
3. He's progréssing very well.
4. He's making excellent prógress.
5. The time for the flight conflícts with my last meeting.
6. There is a cónflict here.
7. The two coastal towns contrást sharply.
8. The cóntrast is very striking.
9. There are many cónverts to the health craze who are eager to convért others.

CULTURE NOTE

Canadians have become very health-conscious. Health food stores can be found everywhere, stocking everything from multi-vitamins to herbal teas. With the fitness craze, sports and fitness clubs have also become popular and many join them not only for exercise, but also to meet people. The government is also encouraging the fitness craze, continuing a program started in the 1970s that had the slogan: "Participaction."

Why this sudden interest? Perhaps there is something in the proverb: "An ounce of prevention is worth a pound of cure." Canadians are learning that a healthier lifestyle leads to fewer medical problems. Heart disease and cancer are only two of the major diseases that have

been linked to diet and lack of exercise.

In addition to a renewed interest in health, Canadians enjoy the benefit of a national health care plan. As a result, the quality of health care in Canada is often considered to be among the best in the world.

Additional Vocabulary

GP—General Practitioner, physician who provides general health care

specialist—physician who specializes in one area of medicine (e.g., plastic surgery, obstetrics, neurology)

clinic—facility where a group of doctors work together outside the hospital

OR—Operating Room where surgery is performed

intensive care—section of a hospital reserved for seriously ill patients who must be carefully watched

ward—section of a hospital (e.g., maternity, pediatrics or cardiac ward)

hypochondriac—person who imagines he or she has an illness

prescription drugs—drugs that are ordered by the doctor, as opposed to over-the-counter medication bought in a drugstore without a prescription (e.g., aspirin)

Discussion Topics

1. What are the advantages and disadvantages of Canada's medicare system?
2. What is your opinion on how to stay healthy and live a long life?
3. Do you believe in folk or herbal remedies? What kinds? Do you have any home remedies for a cold or other common ailment?
4. What is your opinion of your city's smoking by-laws? Are they effective? Should people be allowed to smoke wherever they wish?

Activities

1. In small groups, make vocabulary lists of common medical terms.
2. In pairs, practise various dialogues:

   (a) a doctor-patient discussion on improving the patient's general health
   (b) a reporter interviewing a famous athlete on his or her training program
   (c) a prospective medical student being interviewed by a doctor on why he or she wishes to become a doctor
   (d) someone visiting a friend or relative in the hospital

Assignments

1. Find out about the history of medicare in Canada.
2. Make a list of different kinds of specialists. (Some are listed in the *Yellow Pages* under "Physicians".)
3. Find out about a recreation/sports facility near you and report to the class on the activities offered.

Customs

seven

Customs

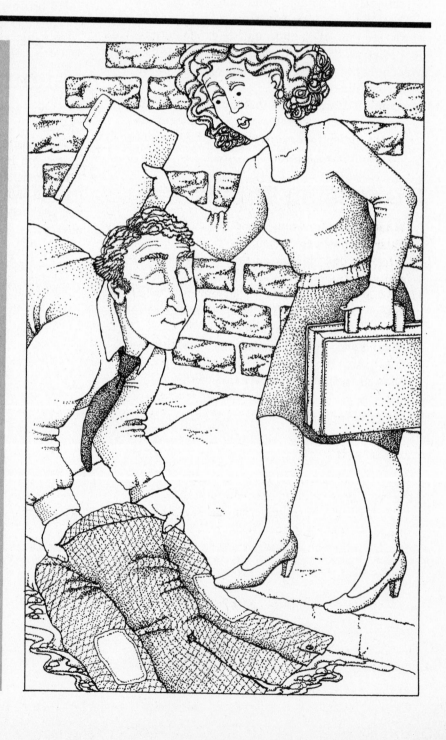

A LETTER TO THE ADVICE COLUMN

Dear Ms. Mannerly,

Now that women are to be treated equally and no longer like fragile objects, I'm **at a loss** when it comes to the everyday **courtesies** I used to extend to them. Is it still correct to open doors and to give up your seat on the bus to women? How about lighting cigarettes for them? I need some **pointers**.

Signed,

Trying not to be a **chauvinist**

Dear Trying,

Common courtesy and practicality are good **rules of thumb**. You should always offer your seat to older or **infirm** people. And while pregnant women are no longer considered infirm, they should still be shown special courtesy. There is no need to offer seats to young, healthy women, just as it is no longer necessary to go out of your way to open doors for them. Open a door for anyone who might have trouble with it—anyone carrying packages or books, for example. Modern young women who want to be treated equally should be prepared to open doors for themselves as well as for other people, male or female.

The same principle applies to lighting cigarettes: if you and a woman are both having a cigarette at the same time, offer the light just as you would to anyone. But don't go **to great lengths**—don't take the matches from a woman to light a cigarette for her if you are not having one yourself. Finally, as in all things, be gracious but be practical.

Sincerely,

M.J. Mannerly

at a loss—confused, unsure of what to do

courtesies—polite or thoughtful acts or expressions

pointers—useful hints or suggestions

chauvinist—man who thinks women are inferior; (original meaning) an overly patriotic person

rule of thumb—(idiomatic) practical rule that has proven useful through experience

infirm—sick, ill

to great lengths—to excess, trying too hard

Mr.

Ms. [Miss
    [Mrs.
[miz]

women [wimmin]

woman

Discussion

1. In your own words, briefly explain the problem and the advice given in this letter and reply.

2. Role play a talk show with classmates. Appoint a team of etiquette experts. Classmates call the experts with various questions, for example:

   Should men stand when a woman enters the room?

   At a very formal dinner, which fork should be used first?

   If a couple breaks up, should they still both be invited to parties by their friends?

   Use etiquette books and newspaper advice columns if you need help.

3. Discuss the statement: "There is much less formality today than there was in the past." How do you feel about the changes in etiquette?

gentle|man|liness

A HOUSEWARMING

wait up—(colloquial) wait for
me

you guys—(slang) term of
address; "guy" usually refers
to a male, but this form of
address can also be used for
females

what's up—what's new, what's
the matter

to have someone over—to have
visitors, or company to your
home

housewarming—party
celebrating a move into a new
home

for good—(colloquial) forever,
permanently, for always

eightish—(colloquial) around
eight o'clock ("—ish" ending
is sometimes used with numbers and adjectives to make
them indefinite, e.g.,
"bluish"— somewhat blue)

a wine 'n cheese—party where
wine and cheese are the main
refreshments (the word
"party" has been dropped
from the end of this
phrase—this explains the use
of the indefinite article)

raincheck—understanding that
an offer will be renewed at
another time

come to think of it—(colloquial)
as I think of it, actually

hang on—(colloquial) wait

Vicky: Hey, **wait up you guys**! I've been looking all over for you.
Irene: Oh, hi Vicky. **What's up**?
Vicky: Well, Steve and I are **having some people over** Saturday night—sort of a **housewarming** party for the new place now that all the drywall and paint have been put away **for good**. Anyway, I was wondering if you two would like to come.
Stan: Oh, that sounds great. What time?
Vicky: Um, **eightish**.
Stan: Can I bring anything?
Vicky: It's basically **a wine 'n cheese** and if you want to bring a bottle—that would be fine. Oh, and dress casually—it won't be anything fancy.
Irene: I'm afraid I won't be able to make it. I'm going out of town for the weekend.
Vicky: That's too bad. I wanted to show you what we've done with the place. You haven't seen it since before the renovations started.
Irene: I guess I'll have to take a **raincheck** on that. Can I get the grand tour some other time?
Vicky: Sure. Why don't you drop by sometime?
Irene: I'll give you a call when I come back. Maybe we can set something up.
Vicky: Oh, and Stan—you do have my address, don't you?
Stan: No, **come to think of it**, I don't. **Hang on** while I get a pen.

Discussion

1. Is this a formal or an informal invitation?
2. Imagine you are the guests at Vicky and Steve's housewarming party. In small groups, talk over your plans (what to bring as a gift, what to wear, how to get there, etc.).
3. Modify the dialogue by changing the type of party and Irene's excuse. Role play the dialogue for the class.

CANADIAN HOLIDAYS

St. Valentine's Day *(February 14th)* is a day to send romantic, sentimental gifts (especially flowers and jewelry) to a spouse or sweetheart. Children often exchange valentine cards. The phrase "Be My Valentine" means "Be my love." The day is symbolized by hearts, flowers, red and pink cards, and Cupid, an angelic child with a bow and arrow.

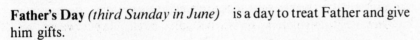

Easter* is usually in April, but the date varies. A four-day long weekend, including Good Friday and Easter Monday, is often given as a holiday from work or school. While primarily a religious holiday commemorating the resurrection of Christ, Easter also means the arrival of spring. Children hunt for Easter eggs hidden by the Easter bunny in and around their home. They colour eggs and are often given gifts of chocolate. Easter supper is traditionally ham, lamb, or turkey. Symbols of Easter include eggs, baby animals (rabbits, chicks, lambs), Easter hats, baskets filled with goodies, and the Easter lily.

Mother's Day *(second Sunday in May)* is a day to treat Mother— breakfast in bed, gifts, flowers, dinner out, and no chores to do (supposedly).

Father's Day *(third Sunday in June)* is a day to treat Father and give him gifts.

Victoria Day* *(the Monday on or before May 24th)* commemorates Queen Victoria's birthday. This long weekend marks the beginning of the summer season for most tourist sites; the season usually ends with the Thanksgiving weekend. Picnics and fireworks are part of the traditional celebrations.

Canada Day* *(July 1st)* marks the day Canada became a country (in 1867), in other words, Canada's birthday. It is celebrated with parades, community picnics, fireworks, and other festivities. The prominent symbol is, of course, the national flag.

Labour Day* *(first Monday in September)* is a holiday in honour of the work force. It coincides with the end of the summer holiday from school.

Thanksgiving* *(second Monday in October)* celebrates the harvest. The traditional meal includes turkey with cranberry sauce, fall vegetables (squash, potatoes), and pumpkin pie. Symbols include harvest vegetables (especially in a cornucopia—horn of plenty), turkeys, and the colourful fall leaves.

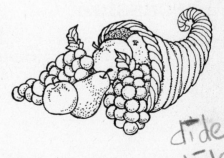

*legal holidays

Halloween *(October 31st)*   is the eve of All Saints' Day when ghosts, goblins, witches, and other supernatural phenomena are supposed to be on the prowl. Children often go door-to-door dressed in costumes, shouting "Trick or Treat," and at the end of the evening, they have bags full of treats (candies). Adults often have costume parties. Symbols include witches, ghosts, jack-o'-lanterns (carved pumpkins with faces), and monsters.

Remembrance Day* *(November 11th)*   commemorates the end of World War I and honours the soldiers who died in the war. War memorials are visited, wreaths are laid at graves, and a minute's silence is observed at 11 a.m. People wear poppies, red flowers with a black centre. It is a day off work and school in some areas of Canada.

Christmas Day* *(December 25th)*   is the most celebrated holiday of the year—celebrations go on for weeks. Christmas is a time for parties, for visits to family and friends, for gift-giving, and for sending cards. Festivities vary according to ethnic and individual family traditions. Traditional foods include turkey, fruit cake, cookies, candies, plum pudding, and many other specialties. There are countless famous songs and stories for Christmas time. Symbols include the Nativity scene commemorating Christ's birth, Santa Claus and his reindeer, stockings filled with gifts, brightly-coloured packages, snowmen, and the Christmas tree with its traditional decorations (bells, stars, angels, candy canes, lights, etc.).

New Year's Eve *(December 31st)*   is a night for partying to "ring out the old year and ring in the new." At midnight people cheer, kiss, toast each other, and sing "Auld Lang Syne." An old man and a young baby symbolize the old and the new year, respectively.

New Year's Day* *(January 1st)*   is usually a time of family get-togethers. It is considered part of the Christmas time celebrations.

While these are the main holidays observed in Canada, there are many other regional and ethnic celebrations in the year.

Discussion

1. Describe other Canadian regional and ethnic celebrations that you are familiar with.

2. In small groups, plan a celebration for the next holiday on the calendar.

LANGUAGE NOTES

Invitations

Generally, the more formal the occasion, the more formal the invitation. Invitations to weddings and formal parties are usually written or printed on special cards. "RSVP" ("repondez s'il vous plait," French for "please reply") is often written on invitations and requires a formal reply.

A formal invitation may be worded as follows:

James Hobson, Mary Hobson-Burke,
and Lynn Hobson
request the honour of your presence
at the 50th wedding anniversary celebration
for their parents
Robert and Gillian Hobson
on Saturday, July 15, 1986, at 6 p.m.
Glenview Community Hall,
598 Barview Place,
North Bay, Ontario   *RSVP*

Compare these examples of informal invitations:

Would you like to come to dinner on Sunday?
Do you want to come over to my place after work?
How about going for a coffee?
Are you doing anything this weekend? We're having a small get-together Saturday night . . .
Hey, if you're not busy, um, I thought we could go out for a pizza tonight . . .

The following expressions may be used to accept an informal invitation:

Thanks, I'd love to.
Okay, sounds good.
That'd be great.
Great, I'll be there.

It is considered polite to give a reason for declining an invitation:

Oh, I'm sorry. I have to visit my family tomorrow.
Sorry, I can't make it today. How about next week?

Thanks for asking but I've made other plans for Saturday.

Many invitations are indefinite:

We should get together sometime for lunch.
Why don't we go over there sometime and check it out?
Drop by sometime.

These invitations are quite casual and are usually followed by a more definite invitation later.

Offers and Requests

Modal verbs such as *can*, *could*, and *would* are often used to make polite requests and offers. Discuss the degree of formality in the following examples.

Offers and invitations:

Can I bring something?
I could do that for you, if you're having trouble.
Can I get you something else? Another cup of coffee, perhaps?
Would you like to go out tonight?
Would you like some more coffee?

Requests and orders:

Can you open the door for me, please?
You can let me off here, thanks.
Could you move your chair a little?
Would you hand me that book?
Would you wait a few more minutes, please?
I would like to look at some sofa-beds.
I would rather watch the movie than the hockey game.

Make the following interrogatives and imperatives into polite offers and requests:

1. Lend me a pencil.
2. Show me some microwave ovens. (to a salesman)
3. Want some cake?
4. Move out of the way.
5. Want to see a movie tonight?

Pronunciation of -s Endings

Endings in -*s* are often difficult for non-native speakers of English to pronounce. These endings occur in the third person singular of the simple present tense (he walks), in plurals (the dogs), in possessives (John's hat), and in contractions (It's time to go now).

The -*s* is pronounced /s/ after voiceless sounds (/p/, /t/, /k/, /f/) and as /z/ after voiced sounds (vowels, /b/, /d/, /g/, /v/, etc.). There should be no vowel sound between the final sound of the word itself and the -*s*.

An extra syllable, however, is pronounced after sibilants. Sibilants, so-called "hissing sounds", are /s/, /z/, /ʃ/, /ʒ/, /tʃ/, and /dʒ/, as in the words *leases*, *amazes*, *wishes*, *garages*, *itches*, and *judges*. In these words, the -*s* ending after the extra syllable is pronounced /IZ/.

Practise the -*s* sounds in the following sentences:

1. Jane's mother wants to plant lilies and tulips in the flower beds.
2. That woman asks the same questions every time she comes here.
3. Tommy's grandfather brings him lots of toys and candies when he visits.
4. Doris' brother loses his keys all the time.
5. He puts tomatoes, onions, radishes, and croutons in the salads.
6. She wishes she could give away all the boxes of clothes and books left behind by her kids.
7. Her conduct always amazes me.
8. She never ceases to make mistakes in her reports.
9. It's been a long time since I've seen fall colours like that.
10. He's very sick; he wheezes and coughs all day.

CULTURE NOTE

Many customs and traditions found in a culture are based on superstition. Superstitions often have interesting explanations, many of which are based on religious beliefs. For example, people say "Bless you" when someone sneezes because it was believed that the soul left the body in a sneeze. Often the original reason has been long forgotten, but the superstition persists. Canadians are not considered to be particularly superstitious, but we have not ruled out superstition altogether.

The number thirteen is considered unlucky in Canadian culture, for example. Friday the thirteenth is an unlucky day and many high-rises do not have a thirteenth floor. At the same time, the numbers three and seven are considered lucky.

Another well-known superstition concerns black cats. If a black cat crosses your path, you can expect bad luck. This fear stems from the Middle Ages when cats were linked to witches and the devil.

It is also considered unlucky to walk under a ladder, open an umbrella in the house, or break a mirror (which is worth seven years' misfortune). A pinch of spilled salt should be tossed over your left shoulder to avoid bad luck. Killing a spider will cause it to rain the next day.

As well, children have their own superstitions. Some are said in rhyme; children going down a sidewalk may chant: "Step on a crack, break your mother's back." Children sometimes pull out the petals of a daisy one at a time saying: "He loves me, he loves me not."

These are just some of the superstitions that are well-known in Canada; they are considered interesting and amusing myths rather than actual rules to live by.

Additional Vocabulary

get-together—informal social gathering or party

BYOB—"Bring Your Own Bottle (or Booze)," please supply your own alcoholic beverage, bring a bottle of wine or whatever you like to drink

TGIF—"Thank God It's Friday," the beginning of the weekend

other celebrations—birthdays, christenings, graduation parties, engagements, weddings, wedding anniversaries

Discussion Topics

1. Describe customs and traditions particular to your culture.
2. Which holiday do you enjoy celebrating most? Why?
3. Can you name any customs that are related to superstition? Are you superstitious?
4. Which Canadian customs do you find different or unusual? Describe any unusual experiences you had when you first learned about these customs.

Activities

1. In pairs and small groups, practise giving, accepting and declining an invitation.
2. In small groups, develop and role play a typical conversation at a family dinner for one of the holidays described.
3. Plan a party for a celebration (such as a birthday, anniversary, or housewarming) and make a list of what has to be bought and what has to be done.

Assignments

1. Consult an etiquette book and newspaper advice columns to find other interesting social do's and don'ts.
2. Look up the history and traditions of various holidays in Canada.
3. Look up other superstitions and their meanings. Which do you find most interesting or unusual? Describe them to the class.

Doris's
the cat's mat
the cats' mat

eight
Love and Marriage

COURTSHIP AND MARRIAGE

Courtship and marriage customs vary considerably from culture to culture. In Canada, the customs tend to reflect the diverse ethnic backgrounds in the country; at the same time, there are definable Canadian customs for courtship and marriage.

Arranged marriages are rare among Canadians. Most people prefer to get to know members of the opposite sex through dating. Steady (or "serious") dating may lead to marriage.

If a couple decides to get married, the two become engaged and the bride-to-be often receives a diamond ring from her **fiancé.** Permission from the parents used to be absolutely necessary; today it is a courtesy to tell the parents first and to ask for their blessing or good wishes. Engagements vary in length depending on the circumstances and the couple's preference.

Once the couple has set the date, they have many decisions to make—whether they want a large or small, traditional or non-traditional, civil or church wedding. Weddings also vary in style depending on the ethnic traditions of the bride and groom.

Before the wedding, the bride may be given a number of "showers" by her friends. During these small (usually all-female) parties, the bride is "showered" with gifts for the home. Friends of the groom **throw a bachelor party** before the wedding day. This is an all-male affair, sometimes called a "stag" party.

On the day of the wedding, it is considered bad luck for the groom to see the bride before the ceremony. The bride usually wears a white gown (a traditional sign of purity) with a veil. She should have "something old, something new, something borrowed, and something blue." The groom often wears a **tuxedo.**

Traditional weddings take place in a church. The groom waits at the altar with the best man. The **ushers** seat the wedding guests. **Bridesmaids** walk up the aisle followed by the bride, who is accompanied by her father. A minister or priest performs the ceremony and the maid (or matron) of honour and the best man act as official witnesses.

The reception after the ceremony is usually a dinner followed by an evening of dancing. The bride and groom greet their guests in a receiving line. While the guests are seated for the meal, there are speeches and **toasts.** When the guests **clink** their glasses with silverware, the bride and groom are expected to stand up and kiss each other. Another important feature of a traditional wedding is the cake; the bride and groom cut the first piece together.

Before the wedding couple leaves the reception, they go to all the guests, thanking them and giving them each a piece of wedding cake to take home. The bride throws her **bouquet** to the unmarried women. The woman who catches it is said to be the next to be married. The groom throws the bride's **garter** to the unmarried men.

Marriages come under provincial **jurisdiction.** In some provinces a blood test is required for a marriage licence. A couple must wait at least three days after the licence is obtained to have the ceremony. Judges or marriage commissioners perform civil ceremonies. Two witnesses are required. A civil ceremony is a legal rather than a religious **rite.**

---

fiancé (m), **fiancée** (f)—(Fr.) man or woman (respectively) engaged to be married
to throw a party—to give a party
tuxedo (or "**tux**")—formal suit
usher—one who escorts guests to their seats (in theatres, churches); male attendant of the groom
bridesmaids—female attendants of the bride
toasts—drinks to honour a person or event
clink—make a short, sharp metallic sound
bouquet—bunch of cut flowers
garter—band or strap worn to hold up a stocking
jurisdiction—extent or range of authority
rite—ceremony

Discussion

1. List some of the features of a traditional wedding in Canada.
2. Discuss other Canadian wedding customs you are familiar with.
3. Compare Canadian wedding customs with those in your culture.

GOING OUT

hard at work—busy, in the middle of working

finish up—complete, conclude

I've really had it—I've had enough, I'm fed up

looks like—looks as if (this use of *like* is considered ungrammatical in formal English)

take in—attend

pick someone up—call at someone's home to give a ride; call on someone

ya—slang form of "you"

(in a library)

Frank: **Hard at work**, I see.

Donna: Oh, hi Frank. Are you here doing that sociology paper too?

Frank: Yeah. I'm just **finishing up** the research today—then I can enjoy what's left of the weekend.

Donna: I know what you mean. **I've really had it** with this place.

Frank: **Looks like** you could use a break. Hey, would you like to go out tonight? I mean, uh, we could **take in** a movie or something. *Citizen Kane* is playing at the Princess.

Donna: Really? You know, I've never seen that movie—I've always wanted to since it's supposed to be a classic. I'd love to go.

Frank: Great. The early show okay? It's at 7.

Donna: Fine.

Frank: You live just off campus, don't you?

Donna: Yeah, about four blocks from here. I'll give you the address.

Frank: I'll **pick you up** around 6:30.

Donna: Better make it a little earlier—there's always a lineup at the Princess.

Frank: Good idea. I'll see you later, then.

Donna: Right. See **ya**.

Discussion

1. In what other ways could Frank have asked Donna for a date?
2. In pairs, develop and role play a dialogue of a different dating situation. For example, Donna asks Frank to come to a dinner party.
3. How do dating customs in Canada differ from those in your country?
4. Do you think it is acceptable for a woman to ask a man out?
5. What do you think of computer dating and other matchmaking services?

THE PERFECT COUPLE

Linda: Keith, you'll never believe what's happened!

Keith: What do you mean?

Linda: Marcia and Harold are getting divorced.

Keith: You're kidding! When? What happened?

Linda: Well, I don't really know, but I heard **through the grapevine** that they've been quietly **separated** for two months already and are filing for divorce. Supposedly they're still **on speaking terms**.

Keith: That's really surprising—I always thought that they were so well **suited to each other**, such similar personalities . . . What about the kids? Who will get **custody**?

Linda: **Joint custody**, I hear. Apparently it's all quite amicable—no **squabbling** over who'll get the house and stuff. An **uncontested** divorce with all the details worked out.

Keith: Boy, that's a change from all the **back-stabbing** you usually hear about . . . I just can't believe it—Marcia and Harold! The perfect couple . . . When will the divorce be final?

Linda: Early in the new year, I guess.

Keith: It just shows how little you know about what goes on in people's lives, doesn't it?

through the grapevine—(idiomatic) through gossip, from other people

separated—legally living apart

on speaking terms—speaking to each other, not hostile

suited to each other—to have similar interests, to be compatible

custody—legal responsibility for the care of the children after divorce

joint custody—shared responsibility

squabbling—(colloquial) arguing

uncontested—undisputed

back-stabbing—(colloquial) betrayal, attack

Discussion

1. Why is Keith surprised?
2. Vary the dialogue by changing the reasons for the divorce and the arrangements. Role play the dialogue variation.
3. Why do you think the divorce rate is so high in modern society?

LANGUAGE NOTES

French Words in English

English has borrowed many words from French. Most borrowings have become anglicized to the point where they are no longer recognizable as French words. Some, however, retain their French spelling (even accent markings) and a modified French pronunciation. French words are often considered elegant and sophisticated; they are especially common in the vocabulary of cooking, dancing, and fashion.

The *é* of the following words is pronounced /e/, similar to the vowel sound of the English word "say":

fiancé résumé sauté cliché flambé pâté

The following words have the same vowel sound /e/ at the end; the final *t* is silent:

bouquet ballet buffet parquet

In these words, the *eau* is pronounced /ow/, similar to the vowel sound in "rope":

trousseau chateau plateau

The *que* at the end of a word is pronounced /k/:

boutique mystique critique

In words that come from French, *ch* is often pronounced like *sh* [ʃ]:

chef chauvinist chateau champagne

Practise the following sentences:

1. To make this *pâté,* you must first *sauté* the chicken livers.
2. The chef at the Chateau Frontenac is famous for his *flambé* desserts.
3. The suite has *parquet* floors.
4. Our relationship has reached a *plateau*; nothing has changed.
5. The medical profession has a certain *mystique* about it.

6. The *ballet* dancer was very selective at the *buffet* table.
7. I have a *rendezvous* with my *fiancé.*
8. You should have a good *résumé* before you go looking for a job.
9. She is out shopping for her *trousseau* and the bridal *bouquet.*
10. In the sixties, every small shop was called a *boutique*; now that term is a *cliché.*

Verbs with *Up*

Up is sometimes added to verbs to strengthen their meaning. Although the verb can be used alone, *up* adds the meaning of *completely.*

I have to *finish up* this research paper today.
I have enough money *saved up* to buy the television set.
Eat up your vegetables or you won't get any dessert.
The documents *burned up* in the fire.
James *cut up* his credit card into little pieces.
She was in a hurry to *open up* the package.
Heat up the soup before serving.

Compose a sentence for each of the following verbs with and without *up*, showing the different meanings:

1. read (up)   4. stand (up)
2. clean (up)   5. walk (up)
3. tear (up)   6. dress (up)

to disguise

CULTURE NOTE

In the past decades, personal relationships have undergone many changes in Canadian society. No longer is the nuclear family the major form of social organization. People are now living together before marriage, entering common-law relationships, staying single, separating, getting divorced, and even setting themselves up as single-parent families. Certainly marriage is still popular with the vast majority of the population, but it is not necessarily a life-time commitment, as divorce statistics indicate.

Marriage today is a choice rather than an obligation. Remaining single used to be a social stigma, especially for women. While the term "bachelor" tends to have the positive connotation of being carefree and enjoying the single life, "spinster" has a negative connotation—often implying an "old maid," someone who is unwanted. Since "Mrs." actually means "married to," women are traditionally known by their husband's name ("Mrs. John Smith"). Today "Mrs. Jane Smith" is a generally accepted form. In fact, many women are also keeping their maiden names after marriage. In response to this, a new term has entered the language—"Ms."—used as a title for both married and unmarried women.

Even in marriage, both husband and wife find that their roles are different from those of their parents. Many couples today choose to remain childless. The husband is also often not the sole breadwinner; many Canadian women hold jobs outside the home. A second income is often an economic necessity. The husband and wife may then share household chores and child-raising responsibilities. Indeed, some husbands choose to stay at home while the wife goes out to work. These househusbands are becoming more accepted.

Additional Vocabulary

marital status—whether a person is single, married, separated, divorced, widowed

blind date—date arranged by a third party for two people who are not acquainted

matchmaker, go-between—intermediary, a person who arranges marriages, or introduces prospective brides and grooms

living together—sharing a residence as a couple, without being married

common-law marriage—non-legalized marriage (used more formally than the term "living together")

marriage of convenience—legal marriage for legal or social reasons, not love

marriage contract—legal agreement between husband and wife outlining domestic responsibilities, marital rights and obligations, and the division of property in the event of a break-up

to stand someone up—to break a date, not to appear at the appointed time and place

going out with someone—dating someone ("dating" is not as commonly used today as are other expressions such as "going out with someone" or "seeing someone")

break-up—separation of a couple

have an (extramarital) affair—be unfaithful to one's spouse

monogamous—to have only one mate

heterosexual—to have sexual feelings for a person of the opposite sex

homosexual, gay—to have sexual feelings for a person of the same sex

Discussion Topics

1. What are the advantages and disadvantages of arranged marriages?
2. Do you think people should live together before getting married?
3. What are the advantages and disadvantages of being married? Of being single?
4. How are marriages today different from those twenty years ago?
5. What do you consider as acceptable public displays of affection? For example, should couples hold hands in public?

Activities

1. Hold a classroom debate on one of the following topics:

   (a) Arranged or traditional marriages are more successful than today's marriages.
   (b) Marriage has little meaning in today's society.
   (c) Men and women should be equal partners in a marriage.

2. In pairs, develop and role play a dialogue in which a couple deals with a domestic situation, such as a financial problem or a problem dealing with the children.

Assignments

1. Find out about the laws and regulations concerning marriages at your city hall, for example, the procedure for getting a marriage licence, the cost, and the facilities for civil weddings.
2. Look through etiquette books and make a list of wedding traditions.
3. Research separation and divorce laws in your province. Report your findings to the class.

nine

Family Ties

THE WORKING MOTHER

greener pastures—(idiomatic) better job or other situation

rat race—(slang) the business world; busy and competitive workplace

tough—(colloquial) hard, difficult

to make ends meet—(idiomatic) to make enough money to pay all living expenses

nanny—live-in babysitter

running herself ragged—(idiomatic) tiring herself out

Superwoman—exceptional woman with above average, superhuman skills

pitch in—help, work together

at any rate—anyway

check out—examine, inspect

peace of mind—calmness, security

Diane: So, I hear Audrey is leaving her job.

Kate: Yeah, she's going on to **greener pastures**.

Diane: Have they found someone to replace her yet?

Kate: No, I don't think so. Why? You aren't thinking of applying, are you?

Diane: Actually, I have been thinking of going back to work. And I wouldn't mind my old job back.

Kate: But I thought you were enjoying life at home.

Diane: It was a nice change from the **rat race**. But now that Jason is almost three—well, it's been **tough** living on one paycheque. It gets harder and harder **to make ends meet**. We're lucky that I could stay home with Jason this long.

Kate: Can you make arrangements for someone to take care of Jason?

Diane: Well, I've been thinking about a daycare centre, or maybe getting a **nanny**. There's a good daycare near here—licensed, trained staff, good facilities . . .

Kate: Being a working mother can be difficult. My sister is **running herself ragged**—getting home after a hard day's work and then trying to do the chores and find some time to spend with the kids . . .

Diane: Well, I have no delusions about being **Superwoman** and Philip and I have talked about splitting chores.

Kate: That's good. It's hard if both partners don't **pitch in** around the house.

Diane: I think I will apply for the job, **at any rate**. And I'll **check out** a few more daycares. I'll have a lot more **peace of mind** about going back to work if we know Jason's getting the best possible care.

Discussion

1. Where might this conversation be taking place? What is the relationship between Diane and Kate?

2. What is Diane planning to do? Why?

3. Many mothers are returning to work before their children are of school-age. What is your opinion of this trend? How can working parents ensure their children's well-being?

4. What are the advantages and disadvantages of mothers holding jobs when they have young children?

5. What responsibilities do husbands and wives share in today's families?

THE GENERATION GAP

George: (answering a knock at the door) Oh, hello Adam. How's it going?

Adam: So-so. I just dropped by to ask you a favour. Could you help us with the moving on Saturday?

George: Moving day already? Sure. No problem. Want some coffee?

Adam: Yeah, okay. Good to sit down for a minute.

George: I guess Teresa and the kids are anxious to get into the new place.

Adam: Yeah, maybe with more room there'll be less **bickering**.

George: Your mother getting to you again?

Adam: Yes, it's been really hard for her to adjust to living with us. She was on her own for so long after Dad died—she misses her independence and is always finding something to complain about. Teresa's been trying to be understanding and considerate, but . . .

George: I know how it is. I wish I could just **declare a truce** with my mother-in-law . . . How are the kids?

Adam: The kids! They seem to be getting more **smart-alecky** all the time.

George: Are they still **giving Teresa a hard time**?

Adam: Yeah, they've been making fun of her English—correcting her all the time. Meanwhile, their Polish is getting so bad—they hardly speak to their grandmother at all.

George: Well, they are in an English environment most of the time.

Adam: It's not like when we were young. They neglect their schoolwork. They seem to be only interested in video games and stereos. Anytime I suggest anything that is constructive, they say "boring."

George: It's just a phase. They'll **grow out of it**. I had problems with Stephanie and Ted too. When they were teenagers, they were the same. But now look at them—I worried for nothing.

Adam: How's Ted doing at university?

George: Not too bad—he's finding it tough going, though. But you know, Stephanie has enrolled her son in **bilingual kindergarten**. Says she wants him to learn about his **heritage**. So now Joey's learning Polish and just a few years ago Stephanie told me that the language was stupid and the culture **backward**.

Adam: Really? I can't believe my kids will ever change that much.

George: Just give them time.

bickering—(colloquial) arguing

declare a truce—make peace

smart-alecky—(colloquial) obnoxious, trying to be smarter than others

give someone a hard time—make it difficult for someone, cause someone a problem

grow out of it—(idiomatic) overcome with time or maturity

bilingual kindergarten—special program in some schools; children learn in two languages in their first year

heritage—what is handed down, or inherited, from ancestors; in Canada, usually one's native culture, an ethnic heritage

backward—belonging to the past, slow in development

Discussion

1. What is the relationship between Adam and George?
2. What family problems do they discuss?
3. Develop and role play a similar dialogue in which friends or relatives discuss a family problem.
4. What does the generation gap refer to? Do you have problems with your parents?
5. Jokes about problems with in-laws are a cliché in North American culture. Discuss relationships with in-laws in different cultures.

LANGUAGE NOTES

Participles

The present and past participles of some verbs are often confused. The present participle is the active form of the regular verb. The past participle is the passive form. This distinction is important to remember; confusing the participles may be misleading and even humorous. "I am boring" (present participle), for example, does not mean the same as "I am bored" (past participle).

Compare the different meanings in the following examples:

I am interested in stamp collecting.
Stamp collecting is interesting to me.
(Stamp collecting interests me.)

I am bored with this class.
This class is boring.
(This class bores me.)

I am confused about this subject.
This subject is confusing.
(This subject confuses me.)

I am excited about going on this trip.
This trip will be very exciting.

I am very tired.
My day was very tiring.

Pronunciation of *-ed* Endings

As with *-s* endings, *-ed* endings are often difficult for the non-native speaker to pronounce. Native speakers do not emphasize the endings and those learning English sometimes do not even hear them and assume they are unimportant. It is important to pronounce *-ed* endings, however, in order to distinguish the past participle and the past tense from other verb forms.

After voiceless consonants, *-ed* is pronounced /t/ as in "backed" and "mopped." After voiced sounds, the ending sounds like /d/ as in "bagged" and "mobbed." This pronunciation is natural, since it is difficult to pronounce two voiced or two voiceless consonants together. However, it is important not to insert a vowel sound. The *e* of *-ed* was pronounced earlier in the history of the English language; today, the vowel sound occurs only when the verb ends in /t/ or /d/ (e.g., wanted, faded).

Practise the following sentences:

1. She is interested in raising a large family.
2. The class is bored with having the same lecture every day.
3. The divorced man walked quickly out of the courtroom.
4. Although Mom and Dad were tired, they skied down the hill again to keep David company.
5. The family couch sagged in the middle and creaked noisily as the kids jumped on top of it.
6. The puppy nipped at his heels and grabbed his pant leg.
7. Even though she rushed, the elderly woman missed the last train.
8. The children huffed and puffed as they climbed the hill.
9. He prodded the dog until it rolled over.
10. I asked my father what he wanted for his birthday.

CULTURE NOTE

The family in Canada is difficult to define because it can vary from the traditional, close-knit, extended family to single-parent families. As well, the average number of children in a family has dropped. Couples may choose to remain childless. The changes in family ties reflect the evolution in social attitudes and the economic environment.

In many cultures, the role of the parent-child bond is quite different than it is in Canada. Here, children are encouraged to be independent. Many young adults leave their family home between the ages of eighteen and twenty-three and live on their own or with their peers. They choose their own career and their own spouse.

Although extended families were common in the past, today few grandparents or aunts, uncles, and cousins live in a multi-generational family. The independence of the elderly is emphasized in Canadian society. A problem may result if a parent is ill and in need of care, however. The children often find it difficult to take an elderly parent into their own home. In Canada, many elderly people live in nursing homes or homes for the elderly and are supported by social security.

Modern family situations can be extremely confusing after marriage breakdowns and re-marriages. Today's children can have several step-parents, step-brothers, and step-sisters. Their lives are often spent going back and forth between the homes of their natural parents. This lack of stability can result in emotional problems.

Another change in family life in the last few years has been an increased awareness of the role of the father. Fathers are spending more time with their children. Most hospitals allow a father into the delivery room so that he can be there to see his children come into the world. From birth, through diaper-changing, to nursery school and extracurricular activities, today's father participates in his children's upbringing; it is not viewed as a solely maternal responsibility.

These confusing changes in family organization have required a re-evaluation of our definition of family. However, social scientists predict that the family unit will stabilize and remain an integral part of society.

Additional Vocabulary

peers—individuals of the same age and social group

toddler—child between the ages of one and three, who has learned to walk but is still rather unsteady

adolescent—teenager in the state of growth from childhood to maturity

only child—child without brothers or sisters

siblings—brothers and sisters

senior citizen—individual over the age of 65

Discussion Topics

1. Why do you think there have been so many changes in family structure?

2. What are the advantages and disadvantages of an extended family?

3. If your elderly parents needed a place to live, would you offer your home? Why or why not? What are the advantages and disadvantages?

4. What do you think of fathers being present when their children are born?

5. "Sibling rivalry" refers to the problems brothers and sisters often have in getting along. What are some common problems? Did you experience these kinds of difficulties? Do you have any suggestions for parents who are trying to minimize sibling rivalry?

6. Some psychologists say that birth order influences personality. For example, firstborns are often independent and have good leadership qualities. Last born children are often spoiled and used to being babied. Do you agree with this? What is your experience?

7. What are some of the childhood stories well-known in your culture? What do these stories say about the culture and the place of children in it?

8. What do you find different about child-raising in Canada?

9. Compare the senior citizens in your native country with those in Canada, in terms of housing, living standards, and family connections.

10. Discuss the advantages and disadvantages of different family groupings (nuclear family, extended family, single-parent family).

Activities

1. Hold a classroom debate on one of the following topics:

   (a) Mothers should not work outside the home.
   (b) Children should look after their elderly parents rather than send them to institutions.
   (c) Adoption records should be open so that children can find their natural parents.

2. Role play the following dialogues:

   (a) parents discussing their child's discipline problems at school
   (b) a teenager asking a parent to use the car
   (c) a couple checking out a daycare centre
   (d) an elderly couple deciding whether to live with their children or in a home for the elderly
   (e) a middle-aged man telling his wife he wants to change his career

Assignments

1. Find out about adoption procedures in Canada.
2. Look up statistics concerning families in Canada (e.g., average number of children per family, number of single-parent families) and report your findings to the class.

ten

Home Sweet Home

HOUSE HUNTING

Emily: Sorry I'm late, Helen. It took a bit longer at the library than I **figured**.

Helen: Oh, that's okay. I'm running late today myself. I just started getting our lunch ready. Did you get anything interesting at the library?

Emily: I picked up a few books on real estate and what you should look for in a house.

Helen: A house? I thought you and Jim were going to wait a couple more years to buy a house.

Emily: We were. But now that interest rates have fallen and since the government has offered all sorts of **incentives** . . . well, it seems like a good time to buy.

Helen: It does look like a **buyer's market** right now.

Emily: But there's so many things to consider. Such a big decision.

Helen: Which part of town are you interested in?

Emily: That's the dilemma. I'd like to live near the university. The houses are so big and they have character. An old house might need a lot of renovation, but I'm quite handy with a hammer and paint brush. We could save money if we did the work ourselves.

Helen: But now that that part of town has become fashionable, people are **flocking** to it, and the prices are really going up.

Emily: That's what Jim says. He'd prefer a new, modern house in the **suburbs**. A lot more affordable.

Helen: They do have all the modern conveniences--extra bathrooms, family rooms.

Emily: But they're so boring. They all look exactly the same and they just sit there on piles of mud. Hardly any stores, no parks.

Helen: All that will come with time—schools, shopping malls, the whole bit. This **subdivision** was just a gravel pit not too long ago, you know.

Emily: But now to buy a brand new house you have to go way out **in the sticks**. And I hate having to **commute** to work every day.

Helen: Well, maybe you two will reach some sort of compromise.

Emily: I suppose so. In the end, it will all depend on our bank account.

Helen: Funny how that always seems to be the **bottom line**.

figured—(colloquial) thought, estimated

incentive—stimulus, encouragement

buyer's market—good market for buyers as opposed to a seller's market, when there is more demand than supply

flock—(idiomatic) gather in a large group, crowd together (used metaphorically—birds travel in a flock)

suburbs—residential areas on the outskirts of a city

subdivision—residential development in the suburbs

in the sticks—(slang) far from the centre of things, the furthest suburbs

commute—travel a long distance from home to work, often from one community to another

bottom line—deciding point

Discussion

1. Where and when is this conversation taking place?
2. What have Emily and Jim changed their minds about and why?
3. Summarize the advantages and disadvantages of a house in the suburbs and one in the city core.
4. Where do you prefer to live?

MOVING OUT

wanna—reduced spoken form of "want to"

getting to me—bothering me

racket—loud noise

res'—abbreviation of "residence"; rooms for students on campus

yuck—exclamation of disgust

didn't sound half bad—(colloquial) sounded quite good

it'll cost a mint—(colloquial) it will be very expensive

scrounge—hunt up, look for

Sally Ann—informal form for Salvation Army—a religious group known for helping the poor; shops where donated, used clothing and articles are sold

thrift shops—second-hand stores

garage sales—private sales in garages to sell used articles people no longer want

dump—(slang) dirty, uncared for place

the Ritz—(idiomatic) fancy, high-class place

out of their hair—(slang, idiomatic) in a position not to bother them

sounds like—sounds as if (ungrammatical use of "like" often heard in informal English)

work cut out—a lot of work to do

(on campus)

David: So, how's it going?

Peter: Not bad. I was just thinking about going back to my room for a coffee—**wanna** join me?

David: Sounds good. Boy, you're lucky having a room right on campus like this.

Peter: I used to think so. But after two years, residence life is **getting to me**. It was great in first year—meeting all sorts of people. But now I think I'd prefer some peace and quiet for a change. All the **racket** in **res'** makes it hard to study.

David: Yeah, I guess so. But it is convenient. And you don't have to cook your own meals...

Peter: You try living on cafeteria food for a while—**yuck!** ... and anyway, what are you talking about—you live at home. You get all your meals home-cooked. I wish my parents lived here—it'd be nice to have all the comforts of home.

David: It's not so great. It's so busy at home—chores to do, so many people coming and going all the time...

Peter: Sounds like you're thinking of moving out yourself.

David: Yeah. I'd like a place of my own. If only it weren't so expensive.

Peter: It's not so bad if you share. How would you like to be roommates?

David: Not a bad idea. I saw some ads for apartments that **didn't sound half bad**.

Peter: But what about furniture and dishes? **It'll cost a mint** just to get set up.

David: I bet my parents would let me have some of the old stuff in the basement. And we could **scrounge** around for other things.

Peter: You mean the **Sally Ann** and **thrift shops**?

David: Sure, and **garage sales**. "Early student" decor.

Peter: Anything'd be better than this **dump**.

David: It won't be **the Ritz**, but it'll be home. And I'm sure my parents'll help me out a bit—anything if it means getting me **out of their hair**.

Peter: **Sounds like** we've got our **work cut out** for us—let's go get a paper and check the ads.

Discussion

1. What is the relationship between David and Peter?

2. What are the advantages and disadvantages of living in a student residence? Of having an apartment?

3. In groups of three, develop and role play a conversation between Peter (or David) and his parents concerning his plans for a place of his own.

4. In small groups, pretend that you are going to become roommates. Make a list of what you will need. Decide on where you are going to live, what articles each person will contribute, and the domestic and financial responsibilities each person will have.

LANGUAGE NOTES

Stress in Sentences

In English, content words, such as nouns and verbs, are stressed; whereas function words, such as prepositions and articles, are unstressed.

In unstressed words, vowel sounds can change. Some are reduced to schwa /ə/. In addition, words such as *a* and *than* sound different in a sentence than when they are said alone. *Than*, for example, sounds the same as *then* in a sentence.

Content words generally receive a single stress. These words include nouns, verbs, adjectives, adverbs, interrogatives, possessive pronouns, and auxiliary verbs contracted with *not*.

Unstressed syllables are difficult for someone learning English to pronounce correctly. If too much emphasis is given the function words in a sentence, the rhythm is destroyed.

Practise the following sentences. Be sure to stress only the marked syllables.

1. John teaches piano to his brother three times a week.
2. I can't understand a word you're saying.
3. There's never any problem with a late brunch on Sunday.
4. I don't want to be late for the get-together.
5. He doesn't speak much English.
6. They'll be here in an hour.
7. I'd rather walk than take that car to the wedding.
8. Why don't you ask him about his ancestors?
9. I found it under the sofa.
10. I can go to the meeting with Jim.

Comparisons

Various comparisons can be used to describe people and things. The comparative and superlative forms of adjectives and adverbs are formed by using *more* and *most* or the endings *-er* and *-est*.

> This book is more expensive than that one.
> He runs faster than Jennifer.
> That is the most outrageous statement I have ever heard.
> He is the tallest boy in the class.

It is important to remember that the definite article must accompany the superlative form. In the comparative, the use of *than* sometimes poses problems because as a function word, it is unstressed in speech and sounds the same as *then* in sentences.

When people are compared, the subject form of the pronoun must be used in formal English:

> Marjorie is younger than *I* am.
> Cathy has more money than *he*.

In informal English, however, the object form of the pronoun is acceptable and is often heard in speech:

> She plays better than *him*.
> Elizabeth swims as fast as *me*.

The pattern *as . . . as* is used to compare things of equal value:

> Matthew is as clever as his sister.
> This story is not as interesting as that one.

In informal English, *like* is often used instead of the proper *as* in comparisons and similes:

> You look like you've been up all night.
> (You look as if you've been up all night.)
> He acts like he knows the way.
> (He acts as if he knows the way.)

Compose sentences comparing:
1. rural and urban lifestyles
2. living in small and large houses
3. renting and owning accommodations
4. living in an apartment and house
5. lifestyles in Canada and in your culture

Use of *House/Home*

A number of idioms in English use the nouns *house* and *home*. While *house* generally refers to a single-family dwelling, *home* is used for any type of dwelling or location (e.g., "I'm going home for the holidays"). *Home* carries an emotional connotation.

House does not always refer to a separate building. It is used in such expressions as: to keep house, to set up house, housekeeper, househusband, housewife. *Home* is used without a preposition in such phrases as: stay home, go home, be home, walk home.

Idioms with *house* and *home*:

The restaurant owner said to his friend: "You'll have to come in and see the new place. Bring some friends and I'll cook a special dinner—*on the house*, of course." (free, paid for by the establishment)

This new job title may sound impressive, but it's really *nothing to write home about*. (not special or impressive)

When I arrived at the apartment, she told me *to make myself at home*. (to make myself comfortable, to act as if it were my home)

CULTURE NOTE

Many Canadians enjoy the luxury of a large amount of living space. Canada is vast, and the homes are large according to the standards of many countries. Even crowded inner cities do not reach the extremes found in other parts of the world.

Canadians appreciate the space and value their privacy. Since families are generally small, many Canadian children enjoy the luxury of their own bedroom. Having more than one bathroom in a house is also considered a modern convenience.

Many rooms in Canadian homes have specialized functions. "Family rooms" are popular features in modern houses; these are, in fact, "living rooms" since many living rooms have become reserved for entertaining. Some homes have formal and informal dining areas, as well.

Recreational homes are also popular with Canadians. Some Canadians own summer homes, cottages, or camps. These may range from a small one-room cabin to a luxurious building that rivals the comforts of the regular residence. Some cottages are winterized for year-round use. Cottages offer people the chance to "get away from it all." They are so popular that summer weekend traffic jams are common, especially in large cities such as Toronto, where the number of people leaving town on Friday night and returning Sunday night blocks the highways for hours.

Sometimes, living in Canada means not only having privacy, but also being isolated. Mobility has become a part of modern life; people often do not live in one place long enough to get to know their neighbours. Tenants live their own lives in their apartments or townhouses. Even in private residential areas, where there is some stability, neighbourhood life is not as close-knit as it once was. There seems to be less of a communal spirit. Life today is so hectic that there is often little time to make friends and to get to know one's neighbours.

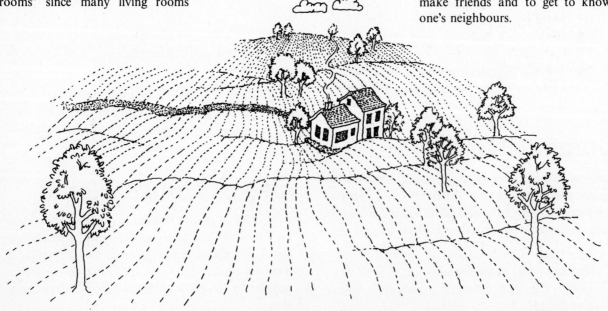

Additional Vocabulary

landlord—someone who lets or rents out property to a tenant; owner of a building

high-rise—building with more than 12 storeys

walk-up—building with no elevator, usually up to 5 storeys

condominium (or, condo)—apartment or town-house that is owned rather than rented; owner usually pays fees to cover maintenance of building and property

mortgage—claim on property given to an individual, bank, or firm for money loaned; loan on a property

Note—Terms for different kinds of buildings may vary from region to region, and even city to city, in Canada. In some places, a "duplex" is a building that contains two apartments; in others, it refers to two houses that are joined and have one common wall. Another example is the use of the word "suite" for an apartment in Alberta; in other areas, such as Ontario, "suite" is used to describe a group of connected rooms in a hotel, but not an apartment.

Discussion Topics

1. Discuss the merits of renting and of owning accommodations.
2. What factors are important when you look for a place to live?
3. Do you prefer city or country living?
4. How do Canadian homes differ from those in your country? How does the type of home affect lifestyle?
5. What do you like and dislike about your neighbourhood?
6. What does it take to be a good neighbour?

Activities

1. In a group, go through the real estate section of your local newspaper. Try to get an idea of the market in your city. Compare the different areas of the city. What kind of rental accommodations are available? What are the costs?
2. In small groups, develop and role play a dialogue of a real estate agent with clients, or of a landlord and a tenant discussing problems.

Assignments

1. Find out about the landlord-tenant laws in your area. Look at various rental applications.
2. Research the community services in your neighbourhood and report your findings to the class.
3. Plan a move into a new home. Make a list of movers or friends you could contact for help and articles you will need.

eleven
Hitting the Books

CONTINUING ED

Paul:	**What'cha doin'?**
Jack:	I'm just trying to decide if I should take a computer course or an accounting course.
Paul:	You goin' back to school?
Jack:	I was just thinking of taking a night course.
Paul:	Why would you want to waste perfectly good evenings sitting at a desk?
Jack:	I don't think they're wasted. I enjoy night courses—you learn new skills, meet new people. Last year I took a **wine appreciation** course.
Paul:	Now that sounds like a good class. But why accounting? Or computers?
Jack:	I **can't get anywhere** at the office—I've got a **dead-end job.** I figure some new skills might help.
Paul:	(looking in the brochure) Hmm... there are some good courses here—"Photography," "Investing in Real Estate," "Public Speaking," and all kinds of languages.
Jack:	So, why don't you take a course too?
Paul:	I just might do that. Here's some cooking courses.
Jack:	Oh, yeah, I can just see it—Paul Barker—**chef extraordinaire.**
Paul:	No, I'm serious. They have one here especially for beginners. I'm getting tired of take-out food and **TV dinners.**
Jack:	Hey, you know, those cooking classes might be a great way to meet new people—especially girls.
Paul:	**Now you're talking.**

what'cha doin'?—(informal) reduction of "What are you doing?"

wine appreciation—wine tasting, a course to learn about different kinds of wine

can't get anywhere—can't make progress or be promoted

dead-end job—job with no future prospects, no hope of promotion

chef extraordinaire—(Fr.) extraordinary chef, great professional cook (used sarcastically in the dialogue)

TV dinners—frozen meals in heat-and-serve trays

now you're talking—(colloquial) that's a good idea

Discussion

1. How old do you picture Jack and Paul to be? Why?
2. If you had the time and the money, what special interest courses would you like to take?
3. Do you want to continue with your education?

ESL CLASS

funny—strange, unusual (the two uses of "funny" are sometimes cleared up by the question "You mean funny ha-ha or funny strange?")

plugging away—(slang) working hard

You can't teach an old dog new tricks—(proverb) as people get older they are less likely to learn new things

cold feet—(colloquial) "to have cold feet" means to be afraid

in the same boat—(idiomatic) in the same situation

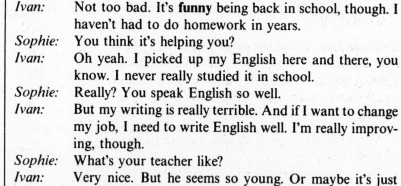

Sophie:	So, how are your English classes going, Ivan?
Ivan:	Not too bad. It's **funny** being back in school, though. I haven't had to do homework in years.
Sophie:	You think it's helping you?
Ivan:	Oh yeah. I picked up my English here and there, you know. I never really studied it in school.
Sophie:	Really? You speak English so well.
Ivan:	But my writing is really terrible. And if I want to change my job, I need to write English well. I'm really improving, though.
Sophie:	What's your teacher like?
Ivan:	Very nice. But he seems so young. Or maybe it's just because I feel so old sitting in a classroom.
Sophie:	Are all the students young, then?
Ivan:	Oh, no. There's one guy who must be close to seventy. And he keeps **plugging away**.
Sophie:	Maybe there's not so much truth in that old proverb—**"You can't teach an old dog new tricks."**
Ivan:	It's hard getting used to this kind of school. I remember school being so strict—everybody sitting in rows quietly doing drills and exercises. Our classroom is so relaxed.
Sophie:	Well, I think it's good you're going to school like that. Just the thought of facing a teacher again gives me **cold feet**.
Ivan:	Oh, it's not so bad. It helps that all the students are **in the same boat**—we're all adults back in school to improve our English.

Discussion

1. What do you think Ivan's English class is like?
2. Why is he studying English?
3. How do you feel about studying English?
4. How are your classes different from those in your country?

LANGUAGE NOTES

You as an Indefinite Pronoun

In casual speech, the pronoun *you* is frequently used instead of *one* as an indefinite pronoun, meaning people in general. It is considered more friendly and much less formal. Compare these examples:

> You can take English classes in the daytime or in the evening.
> One must be careful crossing that street.

This use of the pronoun *you* is also common in proverbs and other expressions such as "you better watch out for . . ."

> Proverb: You can lead a horse to water but you can't make him drink. (You can show someone what is good, but that does not mean that he or she will take advantage of it)

In writing, the use of *you* as an indefinite pronoun is considered incorrect; either the pronoun *one* or an alternate construction, such as the passive, must be used. For example:

> One must begin the process again.
> This article must be read carefully.

There are many common expressions with *you* in English. "You know," for example, can be used in several different ways.

It can be a hesitation marker:

> It's close to that new restaurant—umm, you know—what's the name of the place again?

It is also used to introduce a new fact:

> You know, that place closed down last week.

It can also be used as a request for agreement:

> They really are the best team in the league, you know.

Some people use this expression excessively so that it becomes a verbal tic (involuntary repetition). Avoid over-use of "you know."

Reduction of Sounds

Many verbal expressions, especially those with auxiliary verbs, are reduced in everyday spoken English—"I dunno," for example. Although it is not necessary for those learning English to use these reduced forms, it is important to be able to understand them.

Vowel sounds are omitted and consonant sounds are merged in the process of contraction and ellipsis (omission of words or sounds). These reductions occur only in speech, but written forms are used in dialogues or plays to show the pronunciation. Compare these examples:

I don't know	I dunno
have got to	gotta
going to	gonna
want to	wanna
have to	hafta
supposed to	s'posed to
ought to	oughta
could have	coulda

Other very informal reduced forms include:

What are you doing?	What'cha doin'?
How did you do it?	How'dja do it?

CULTURE NOTE

Many different kinds of educational opportunities are available to Canadians. Education is under provincial jurisdiction and school regulations therefore vary from province to province. By law, children between the ages of five and sixteen must attend school. Most students, however, go on to complete high school and they are then generally eighteen years old. Public elementary and secondary schools are available with no tuition costs. In addition, there are separate school systems for Roman Catholics, and many private schools which can have various teaching philosophies. Private schools require tuition fees.

Post-secondary schools include colleges and universities. Usually, colleges are vocationally oriented; whereas universities offer wider-based academic studies, as well as training for various professions (law, medicine, teaching, engineering, etc.). While there are tuition fees, colleges and universities receive most of their funding from both the federal and provincial governments.

No longer is education basically for children and young adults. Adult education is a growing field. Adults already in the work force often go back to school to re-train or to upgrade their skills. Many special interest courses that are not career-oriented are also available. Canadians can improve their education through night courses, on-the-job training, summer institutes, weekend workshops, or correspondence courses.

Depending on the kind of course, the teaching-learning environment can vary considerably. Instructors may prefer an informal atmosphere, where student participation is a major component of the class. Other instructors may prefer a more traditional lecture kind of atmosphere, where students play a more passive role. Similarly, the class atmosphere can vary from being highly competitive to being more cooperative and supportive.

The modern Canadian educational system generally stresses independent study, creativity, and the application of knowledge over the recital of facts. This emphasis can sometimes pose a problem for students who are accustomed to a system in which learning by rote or memorization is stressed. The image of a good student can also vary—to some it is someone who works quietly and conscientiously and shows respect for the teacher; to others it is someone who expresses his or her own opinion.

With the wide variety of educational programs and a general awareness of the benefits of learning, many Canadians view education as a life-long pursuit.

Additional Vocabulary

nursery school—school for children under the age of five

elementary school—Kindergarten and Grades 1 to 6 or 8

junior high school—Grades 7 to 8 or 9

secondary school, high school—Grades 9 to 12 or 13

seminars—small discussion groups

workshop—class where students have an opportunity to practise skills

degree—rank or title given by a university to a student who fulfills particular requirements

Bachelor's degree—(B.A., B.Ed., B.Sc., etc.) first university degree attained after three or four years of study

Master's degree—(M.A., M.Sc., etc.) university degree acquired after a Bachelor's degree

Ph.D. or doctorate—third university degree, entitles graduate to use the title "Dr." before the last name

undergraduate—student working on his or her first degree (Bachelor)

graduate student—student working on a Master's or Ph.D.

correspondence course—home-study course; materials and assignments are mailed out

tutor—private teacher or assistant teacher

Discussion Topics

1. Compare the Canadian educational system with that in your country.
2. What is your opinion of university and college admission requirements for foreign students?
3. What are the general benefits of education?
4. What are the advantages and disadvantages of being a teacher?
5. How are computers changing education today? What are the advantages and disadvantages of using computers?

Activities

1. In pairs, develop and role play a dialogue in which a student and a counsellor discuss problems with course changes, marks, or career decisions.
2. Hold a classroom debate on one of the following topics:

   (a) A university education should be available to everyone at minimal or no tuition fees.
   (b) A child's education should be determined by the parents and not by the government.
   (c) Standards of education should be stricter.

3. In small groups, design the ideal school by listing ten important characteristics.

Assignments

1. Find out about the different educational institutions in your city and what they offer in post-secondary and general interest programs.
2. Look through college and university calendars to find out what kind of programs they offer.

twelve
Language

A BROADCAST INTERVIEW

Interviewer:	And now we have an interview with Professor J.T. Lingo, a professor of **linguistics** at Chimo University, who is here to talk to us about the growing business of teaching English. Good morning, Professor Lingo.
Professor:	Good morning.
Interviewer:	Professor, I understand that teaching English is becoming "big business" all around the world.
Professor:	Yes, indeed. It seems that language schools are springing up everywhere and that a lot of Canadians are going overseas to teach English.
Interviewer:	Why is that?
Professor:	Today English is one of the most important languages in the world. It is the language of business, aviation, science, international affairs, and even pop culture.
Interviewer:	Pop culture?
Professor:	Yes, in many countries rock 'n roll songs are sung in English. Sometimes the singers barely understand what they are singing.
Interviewer:	And do these people find English an easy language to learn?
Professor:	Well, every language has something about it that other people find difficult to learn. English is such a **hodge-podge** of different languages—it's essentially Germanic, but a lot of its vocabulary comes from French, and technical words stem from Latin and Greek. This feature makes English fairly adaptable—which is a good thing for a world language, or **lingua franca**, as we say—but it also **plays havoc** with spelling and pronunciation.
Interviewer:	English spelling **baffles** me too. That's why I'm a **broadcaster** and not a **print journalist**. (laughs)
Professor:	Yes, well, anyway, English also has the largest vocabulary. Often there are two words for the same thing, one that is Anglo-Saxon and one from the French—like "buy" which is Anglo-Saxon and "purchase" which is from the French. The French word often has more prestige.
Interviewer:	Anglo-Saxon?
Professor:	That's the word for Old English. The **Norman conquest** in 1066 brought the French language to Britain and helped English evolve into the language it is today.

cont'd

linguistics—scientific study of language
hodge-podge—(colloquial) mixture
lingua franca—(Latin) world language, language used between people speaking different native languages
plays havoc—ruins, causes destruction
baffles—confuses
broadcaster—announcer on radio or TV
print journalist—journalist working in newspapers or magazines
Norman conquest—victory of William the Conqueror, from France, over Britain

slang—language not suitable
for formal use; words and
expressions often short-lived
or particular to a certain
group
colloquial—everyday, informal
language
dialects—variations of the same
language

Interviewer:	I see. Is there anything else particularly difficult about English?
Professor:	Well, the idioms in informal English pose a problem for some students.
Interviewer:	Informal English?
Professor:	As with any language, there are different varieties—**slang**, **colloquial**, formal, written—as well as the different **dialects**—British, American, and Canadian English.
Interviewer:	And how is Canadian English different from American and British?
Professor:	Well, Canadian English is closer to American in pronunciation and idiom. Some of our words and spellings do reflect British usage, however. We wouldn't use the British term "lorry" for truck, but we have kept the "our" spellings in words such as "honour" and "colour."
Interviewer:	This has been very interesting, professor. I'm afraid we're out of time. It has been a pleasure talking to you.
Professor:	Thank you.
Interviewer:	We have been talking to Professor Lingo of Chimo University. And now back to Barbara.

Discussion

1. Do you agree with Professor Lingo's assessment of the importance of English and its relative difficulty?
2. Do you think there will be one world language? Will it be English?
3. How does English influence other languages and cultures?

LEARNING BY EXPERIENCE

Tony: Hello Maria. My brother home yet?

Maria: No, but he should be here any minute. Have a seat. How was work today?

Tony: Pretty good. I think I'm starting to make friends. Some of the guys asked me if I wanted to go out with them tonight. They said they were going to do some painting, but I said I was too tired.

Maria: Painting? On a Friday night?

Tony: Yeah, painting something red, I think they said.

Maria: Oh—"painting the town red." It's an old idiom—it means going out for a good time.

Tony: Now it makes sense. I really have trouble understanding them sometimes. English is a crazy language—so many idioms. Why can't they just say what they mean?

Maria: Every language has idioms, Tony.

Tony: But English is so illogical. There aren't any rules. It doesn't make sense. Spanish is so easy and clear.

Maria: Sure—to native speakers of Spanish. Don't worry— English isn't that hard. You'll **catch on** to what people are saying.

Tony: **One of these years.**

Maria: I remember my first few days in Canada. One time I was standing at a bus stop and a woman asked me how long I'd been there and I said three weeks. She gave me a funny look and didn't say anything. I thought she was rude, but now I realize she was just asking me how long I had been at the bus stop. I was so used to people asking me how long I had been in Canada, that I had answered automatically.

Tony: That's not all that embarrassing.

Maria: But that's not the only time I misunderstood someone. Those first few months were filled with mistakes and misunderstandings. Even though I'd studied English in Portugal, people here just didn't talk the way I had been taught.

Tony: Maybe I should just throw out my grammar books and **start from scratch**.

Maria: I wouldn't go that far. I just think you have to listen to people talking as well as study from books.

catch on—understand, see the significance of

one of these years—(idiomatic) it will take a long time; it will seem like forever

start from scratch—start with nothing

Discussion

1. What is the probable relationship between Tony and Maria?
2. What experiences have they had learning English?
3. Describe a personal experience that became very comical because of a communication problem.
4. When and how did you start learning English? What experiences have you had in your study? What do you find hardest to master in English?

LANGUAGE NOTES

Narrative Techniques

Conversations often include narratives and short stories or anecdotes, relating something which happened to the speaker or something which the speaker heard about. These stories serve to give an example or to entertain the audience.

Just as different cultures have different writing styles, they also have different story-telling techniques. English is a concise language, and the style is often brief and to the point. Some cultures, on the other hand, favour embellishment and indirectness in a narrative style.

A story should suit the situation and make a point that will add to the conversation.

A story can be introduced by such phrases as:

You'll never guess what happened . . .
That reminds me of the time . . .
You know, once . . .
I remember when . . .

The second important element is a description of the setting. The listener needs enough information to understand the situation, but unnecessary details should be left out. The setting includes the place and time that the story takes place. The listener forms his or her expectations about the story from the setting. For example, from the phrase "when I first started my new job," the listener will expect the story to include characters from work and to tell of the story-teller's new experiences on the job.

In order to give enough information, but not too much, it is important to test the knowledge of the listener through such expressions as:

You know that new restaurant on Main Street? Well . . .
It was in Calgary—have you ever been there?
I was talking to John yesterday—have you met him?

The characters of the story should also be described in as much detail as is necessary.

Some pauses in a story are effective to create suspense. The following phrases are common:

And you'll never guess what happened next . . .
And then—and I still don't believe this—he said . . .

To shorten details of a story, the following phrases can be used:

Well, to make a long story short . . .
I won't go into all that, but . . .

Listen to other phrases and techniques that speakers use to tell a story. Practise these techniques in class activities and discussions. Effective story-telling is an art, and can add interest to a conversation.

Reported Speech

When telling a story, speakers often use forms of indirect or reported speech instead of quoting directly. When the verb in the main clause is in the past tense, it is necessary to change the tense of the original speech. Compare the following examples of direct and indirect speech:

John asked, *"Are* you coming?"
John asked if we *were* coming.
Peter said, "I *want* to go to the library tomorrow."
Peter said that he *wanted* to go to the library tomorrow.
Susan asked, *"Have* you been here long?"
Susan asked if I *had* been here long.
Harry said, "We *will* be late."
Harry told her that they *would* be late.

If the verb in the main clause is not in the past tense, the tense of the original speech does not change:

She says, "I'll be going now."
She says that she'll be going now.

Similarly, for facts that are generally true, the tenses are not changed:

She said, "English is hard to learn."
She told me that English is hard to learn.

Change the following quotes into indirect speech and the indirect speech into direct quotes.

1. "Help, I need a hand!" Ken yelled.
2. Doug stated that he was tired of commuting between two cities.
3. "Come and get it!" cried the cook at the barbecue.
4. Barbara laughed and suggested that her brother should stop having so much fun and instead work a bit harder.
5. "Make sure your spelling is accurate in the essay," stated Simon.

CULTURE NOTE

Language is an important issue to Canadians. Since Canada has two official languages—French and English—Canadians are entitled to information and services from the federal government in either language. For example, Canadians have the right to use English or French in federal courts.

The Canadian government has sought to ensure the status of both languages through the Constitution Act. Due to the overwhelming influence of English, it was thought that French was in danger of dying out in North America. Laws in this country now reflect this concern.

In Québec, the Commission de la langue française regulates the use of French in the province. It demands that official signs and documents be in French, that the use of anglicisms in the language be controlled, and that French language studies be encouraged. Education in French for francophone children is a major concern across the country. Many anglophone children are also being educated in French, thus fostering the growth of the French language in Canada.

In addition, many Canadian Indians have preserved their native languages. Several native languages, however, are now in danger of dying out. To encourage their use, some education systems offer studies in languages such as Cree and Algonquin.

Immigrants in Canada have also introduced a variety of languages. Again, many education systems offer second languages so that the children of immigrants can keep this important aspect of their heritage. Succeeding generations often lose fluency in their mother tongues since they study and live in a predominantly English or French environment outside their homes. Canadians who feel a tie with their ethnic background often study their ancestral languages.

Thus, although English is an important language in the world, second language study is encouraged in Canada. Children may begin learning a second language as early as kindergarten or nursery school. Adult education centres also offer courses in a variety of second languages and various special language schools are flourishing across the country. In general, Canadians recognize the value of speaking more than one language.

Additional Vocabulary

francophone—French-speaking

anglophone—English-speaking

immersion classes—classes in which students are completely surrounded by or "immersed" in another language and culture

registers—different levels of language (e.g., formal, casual)

jargon—specialized, often technical, words used in a particular profession (e.g., legal jargon)

idiom—phrase or expression, the meaning of which cannot be understood from the meanings of the individual words

anglicize—to make or become English in form, pronunciation, or character

Discussion Topics

1. If you could learn another language, which would you choose and why?
2. Compare two languages that you are familiar with in terms of relative difficulty, use of idioms, or similar pronunciations, for example.
3. What anglicisms appear in your native language? What do you think of this phenomenon?
4. In many countries, one particular dialect becomes the national language. Many factors influence this process. Sometimes an official government decree establishes the national language. In China, for example, Mandarin is considered the official language, while the use of other dialects, such as Cantonese, is discouraged. In African countries, an official language sometimes has to be chosen by the government. These situations can create conflicts. Discuss the issue of language planning and the role of government.
5. Discuss the use of French and English in Canada. Do you know of other countries that have more than one official language? What are the advantages and disadvantages?
6. Does becoming bilingual change a person? In what way?
7. Do you think children of immigrants should be encouraged to keep their mother tongue?

Activities

1. Hold a classroom debate on one of the following topics:

   (a) There should be an official agency to set rules for standard English.
   (b) There should be only one official language in Canada.
   (c) An artificial language, such as Esperanto, which is based on words from the chief European languages, should be made the *lingua franca*.

2. Try to learn a phrase or expression, such as "Good day," in each different language that is spoken in the class.

Assignments

1. Make a list of ten words that have entered the English language in the twentieth century.
2. Find out more about the laws governing the use of French and English in Canada and in your province.

thirteen
Travel and Tourism

SIGHTSEEING

cooped up—(slang) confined, locked up

hit-or-miss—haphazard, careless

browsing—looking around without a specific purpose, for enjoyment

Scene: Ottawa, an outdoor café on the Sparks Street Mall. A couple (Brian and June) is sitting at a table looking over maps and tourist brochures. A second couple (Lynn and Bill) is sitting nearby.

June: I don't know, Brian. There's just so much to see and so little time.

Brian: Well, we do have to make up our minds. This afternoon we could go to see the National Gallery or the Museum of Man or . . .

June: It's too nice a day to be **cooped up** in an old museum.

Brian: Well, let's see what else we could do . . .

Bill: Excuse me, we couldn't help noticing that you're new in town. Do you need any help?

Brian: It would be nice to get a personal opinion on some of this stuff. The brochures make everything sound so terrific.

Lynn: I know what you mean. Sightseeing can be such a **hit-or-miss** thing.

June: We'd like to do something outdoors, but not just wander around aimlessly.

Bill: Have you seen the old market area yet? It's my favourite part of the city—a lot of renovated historical buildings and reconstructed courtyards with different shops, boutiques, market stalls . . .

Lynn: You know, they have free guided walking tours of the area—a nice way to get an introduction to a place. Then you can stay and do some **browsing** on your own afterwards.

June: That sounds like a great idea. It would be nice to have a guide to explain things, instead of always looking up the information in a brochure.

Brian: So where do these tours start?

Bill: Right in front of the Parliament Buildings. Just go up Sparks two blocks, turn left on Metcalfe, and there should be signs on the corner of Metcalfe and Wellington.

Brian: Great, thanks a lot.

Discussion

1. Why do you think Bill and Lynn knew that Brian and June were new to the city?
2. Is a walking tour a good way to see a city? How do you like to get to know a new place?
3. Change the location of this dialogue so that it is in your city or region. Make the necessary changes and perform it for the class.
4. In pairs, practise giving directions to various places. Use different kinds of maps (province, city, campus, buildings) to help you.

A TRIP TO THE WEST COAST

Robin: Oh, hi Julie. Finally back from your vacation, I see.

Julie: What do you mean, "finally"? I feel like I've only been gone for two days instead of two weeks.

Robin: Well, **you know what they say**—**"time flies** when you're having fun." You did have fun, didn't you?

Julie: Oh, it was marvelous. B.C. is so beautiful. And it was so nice to get away from this cold, miserable weather. And those mountain views—they were absolutely **breathtaking**.

Robin: How was Vancouver?

Julie: Busy. So much to see and do there. I hadn't realized how much I missed big-city life after **being stuck** out here in the **boonies** for so long (laughs).

Robin: So what all did you do?

Julie: Oh, we went to Stanley Park and the aquarium, up Grouse Mountain, and to museums and galleries. All the usual **touristy** things.

Robin: Did you get over to the island? It's only two hours away by **ferry**, isn't it?

Julie: Yes, it was funny how on the ride over everyone stayed out on deck to enjoy the view, but on the way back, we just sat inside like **seasoned travellers** and read magazines!

Robin: Victoria is a city I've always wanted to visit. They say it's such a quiet and elegant city with a lot of British influence.

Julie: We liked Victoria so much that we stayed on a day longer than we'd planned. I did like the custom of afternoon tea—it was a nice break from sightseeing too.

Robin: Oh, well, one of these days I'll get there myself. In the meantime, **I better** get back to work. Maybe we can get together sometime and you can tell me more about it.

Julie: Sure, and I'll show you my pictures once I get them developed.

Robin: Great. See you later.

Julie: Bye.

you know what they say—expression used to introduce a saying or proverb; "they" refers to people in general

time flies—time goes by quickly

breathtaking—exciting or wonderful

be stuck somewhere—(colloquial) be unable to move or go anywhere else

boonies—(slang) "boondocks," far from big-city life

touristy—slang adjective form of "tourist"

ferry—boat which transports cars and people

seasoned travellers—experienced travellers

I better—reduced spoken form of "I'd better"

SEAQUEEN TOURS

Discussion

1. Where do you think this dialogue is taking place? What is the probable relationship between Robin and Julie?

2. Has Robin ever been to the west coast of Canada?

3. Change the dialogue so that Julie has just come back from a visit to a city near where you live. Practise different variations of the dialogue in pairs.

4. Give a short oral presentation to the class on a place you have visited or a place you would like to visit.

LANGUAGE NOTES

Tag Questions

Tag questions are interrogatives attached to the end of a statement. They request agreement or confirmation:

> That was a good concert, *wasn't it?*
> The bus leaves at seven, *doesn't it?*

Tag questions are formed with the auxiliary verb (or the verb *to be*) and a pronoun subject.

The tags for "I am" and "let's" are not regular:

> I'm invited too, *aren't I?*
> Let's go, *shall we?*

It is important to use a contraction in a negative tag question. Uncontracted forms are rare and sound very formal.

A tag question is used to make polite conversation. It requires a yes or no answer and is often used where a direct question would be inappropriate:

> It's a nice day, isn't it?
> The band plays well, doesn't it?

When a tag is simply asking for agreement, the intonation is rising-falling as in standard statements.

Sometimes the speaker uses a tag to get confirmation of a fact he or she is not quite sure of:

> It's two hours by ferry, isn't it?

In this case, the rising question intonation is used.

Add tag questions to the following sentences:

1. Pamela has travelled to Korea and Japan.
2. The Bach Festival was simply marvelous.
3. The plane leaves before noon.
4. There are several different routes to Yellowknife.
5. Retirement is a great time to plan a trip around the world.
6. Joseph spends half this time of year in Victoria.
7. The bus will be late.

Word Stress

Stress of multi-syllabic words in English is often a problem. There is no one regular stress pattern and since English words come from so many different sources, a particular stress often has to be learned with each new vocabulary item. Misplacement of a primary stress can often make a word unrecognizable. If you are unsure, check a dictionary. Word entries usually mark the primary stress. Unstressed syllables in English have a reduced vowel sound. Many unstressed vowels are pronounced /ə/ (schwa).

Practise the following Canadian place names. The primary stress is marked for each word.

Cánada	Saskátchewan	Torónto
Hálifax	Albérta	Óttawa
Chárlottetown	Vancoúver	Montreál
Ontário	Édmonton	Newfoúndland
Manitóba	Wínnipeg	or Newfoundland

CULTURE NOTE

Tourism is a major industry in Canada. Canada is a vast country and there is enormous variety within its boundaries. Since the country is so large, Canadians are used to travelling long distances, even for a weekend. But because it is difficult to see all that the country has to offer, Canadians sometimes find it easier and cheaper to travel outside the country, especially to the United States.

Ironically, Canadians are often more aware of the tourist areas far from home than those nearby. Many Canadians live in a city for years without seeing the local museums. Others only visit local sites when they have out-of-town visitors to show around their area.

During the winter, thousands of Canadians flock to warmer climates for vacations. Florida, California, Hawaii, Mexico, and the Caribbean are popular winter vacation areas. European holidays also appeal to many Canadians, who find the contrasts between the "old country" and the "new world" fascinating.

Within Canada, vacationers are

offered a wide range of holidays. Some are lured by the wilderness. Canadians take pride in the varied landscape and climate: the barren north, the mountains of the west, the coastal fishing villages, the huge expanse of the prairies. Camping and hiking are popular outdoor activities and avid sportsmen are attracted to the Canadian outdoors.

The urban areas in Canada are interesting contrasts to the "great outdoors" and reflect the common attractions of populated areas. Vacationers enjoy all the advantages of city life—the theatre, galleries, restaurants, libraries, and clubs. Canadian cities enjoy a reputation for cleanliness and for an abundance of greenery. Each Canadian city has something different to offer. There are the old world sections of Québec City and the national museums of Ottawa, the modern western flavour of Calgary and the stately charm of Victoria.

Additional Vocabulary

People get on a bus · · · · · · People go by bus
       on a train · · · · · · · · · · · · · · · by train
       on a plane · · · · · · · · · · · · · by plane
       on a ship · · · · · · · · · · · · · · by ship
   but in a car · · · · · · · · · · · · · · by car
       in a taxi · · · · · · · · · · · · · · · by taxi
                                    on foot

board—get on a ship, train, plane, bus
disembark—leave a ship, plane
deplane—leave an aircraft
taxi—go along the ground under an aircraft's own power before or after flying (before "lift-off" or after "touch-down")
check in, check out—official arrival and departure in a hotel
hitchhike—travel by asking for rides from motorists along the road; "to thumb a ride" (slang)

motel—roadside hotel or group of cottages for people travelling by car (often with a separate entrance for each room)
inn—hotel, often a small hotel (used in names, e.g., "The Convention Inn")
hostel—lodging for travellers, usually members of a hostelling organization (often does not have individual rooms and bathrooms)
resort—holiday or vacation area, usually at a beach or in the mountains
cruise—pleasure trip on a boat or ship
return trip—two-way trip (there and back); round trip

Discussion Topics

1. What are the benefits of travel? What are some of the difficulties?
2. If you could travel to any place in the world, where would you go for a holiday?

3. Would you prefer an extended or a short holiday? Why?
4. What tips would you suggest to a new traveller?
5. Describe some of your more humorous travelling experiences.
6. What tourist sites are you familiar with in your city or area?

Activities

1. In pairs or small groups, develop and role play a dialogue in which you are asking a travel agent for the following information:

   (a) a flight to Paris, France
   (b) a reservation on a bus tour to Jasper, Alberta
   (c) reservations in Vancouver, B.C.
   (d) an inexpensive flight out of New York to London
   (e) a berth on a transcontinental train

2. Make a short presentation to the class describing a region in Canada. Use brochures and pictures from books in your presentation.

Assignments

1. Plan a short trip around your province, highlighting places of interest. Obtain information from the tourist office or travel agent to help you make a detailed plan.
2. Visit a travel agent and find out about various kinds of holidays (cruises, safaris, bicycle tours). Describe the holidays to the class.

fourteen
Running the Country

RED TAPE

benefits—money paid to the sick, disabled

Workers' Compensation—board which pays people injured on the job while they are off work

run-around—(slang) series of excuses, evasions, or deceptions; not getting the right answer from anyone

validate—confirm, verify

blasted—exclamation of anger or disgust; mild swear word

paperwork—clerical work; filling out forms

red tape—excessive rules and regulations made by a company or the government (so-called because official documents used to be tied with red tape)

Clerk: May I help you?

Dan: Yes, I was told that I could renew my application for **benefits** from **Workers' Compensation** here.

Clerk: That's right. I'll get you a form.

Dan: What a relief! I've been getting the **run-around** all day—this is the third office I've been to.

Clerk: Here you are. Fill out this form with the information about your original claim and then take it to the Social Services and Community Health Department. They will **validate** your claim for additional assistance while you're off work ... And this form is for the Department of Hospitals and Health Care ...

Dan: All this **blasted paperwork**! I've heard about **red tape** but this is ridiculous! One last question. I'm hoping that this month will be my last one for benefits. When I'm finished, how do I let my boss know that I'm officially ready to go back to work?

Clerk: Well, there's another form put out by Workers' Compensation. It requires a doctor's recommendation, one of the Compensation doctors.

Dan: Great. I hate to ask, but where do I pick that up?

Clerk: You can get it right here. Here you go. If you have any problems with the form—just ask me.

Dan: Thanks, you've been a real help. See you later.

Discussion

1. What conversations might Dan have had at the other two offices he visited?

2. Practise variations on the dialogue by changing the information requested (e.g., an application for a federal grant, information about maternity leave benefits, or something you have had to deal with).

3. What successes and problems have you had dealing with various government agencies?

4. In groups, suggest ways to look for information on the following topics:

   (a) medicare payments
   (b) energy resources in the province
   (c) utility rates
   (d) parking laws on city streets
   (e) pension plan payments

MEET THE MAYOR

(on television)

Interviewer: Mr. Mayor, I understand you are planning to run for office again in the up-coming **municipal** election.

Mayor: That's right. I've served as mayor of this city for four years and I feel that **my record stands for itself**. A lot of good has come to this city during my term!

Interviewer: What about **allegations** that the city is way **over budget**?

Mayor: I admit we have had some **setbacks**. The construction strike put us behind schedule with many of our projects, especially with the new convention centre. But none of this could have been foreseen.

Interviewer: Will the business generated really justify the enormous costs of the convention centre?

Mayor: Certainly, we have already seen indications—we've booked several major conventions.

Interviewer: What about the rumours of **discord** on council?

Mayor: I admit we had some problems at first, but I think they're all **ironed out**. And I understand that most of the **councillors** will be seeking re-election.

Interviewer: What do you see as the major issues in this election?

Mayor: Without question, unemployment and the economy are everyone's major concern and I intend to deal with those issues. I consider myself a **grassroots** politician.

Interviewer: Do you think that you will be a **shoo-in** to win the election simply because you're the **incumbent**?

Mayor: No, I intend to campaign hard in this election and not simply **rest on my laurels**. And I believe that the voters are satisfied with what I have accomplished and will re-elect me.

Interviewer: Thank you Mr. Mayor.

municipal—city
my record stands for itself—my record does not need explanation or excuse
allegations—assertions without proof; accusations
over budget—over the cost allowed for
setbacks—reversals or delays
discord—disagreements, arguments
ironed out—(idiomatic) smoothed out, solved
councillors—elected municipal representatives
grassroots—concerning the people, the voters
shoo-in—(colloquial) a sure thing; easy or certain to succeed
incumbent—person holding office
rest on my laurels—(idiomatic) pause to enjoy the fame earned by my work (a laurel wreath was the victor's crown in ancient Greece)

Discussion

1. What main problems has the mayor faced in his term of office?
2. In pairs, develop and role play an interview with a politician or celebrity.
3. Make a short presentation to the class about a particular agency or department of the government.

NEWS BROADCASTS

alleviating—lessening, relieving

leadership review—critical review of a political party leader's capabilities and past performance

leaked—released (as in confidential information)

anonymous—unidentified

task force—governmental group formed for a specific objective

quotas—certain number of individuals, a share of a group

affirmative action—employment programs to hire individuals from minority groups experiencing discrimination

"A special party convention on the economy has been called for early in the new year. Proposals for **alleviating** high unemployment and interest rates will be considered. In addition, party unity and the up-coming **leadership review** will be debated. High-ranking members of the party are expected to attend."

"The Minister of Communications denied that budget cuts will be made in the new year. But government memos **leaked** to the press today indicate drastic cuts in personnel and resources. A senior official in the government, who asked to remain **anonymous**, stated that the budget cuts would be restricted to regional offices. The Minister will make a statement tomorrow."

"The provincial government in Newfoundland is planning to construct regional hospitals in many rural communities. These additional hospitals will allow everyone in the province equal access to health care. However, the Medical Commission has objected to the plans on the basis that it is difficult to attract doctors to rural communities."

"A recently released **task force** report on employment has recommended reforms targeted at women, minority groups, and the disabled. This report recognizes the problems inherent in legislated **quotas** for employment or promotion. Instead of demanding **affirmative action** programs, however, it recommends that the Human Rights Commission be given new powers to encourage employment for disadvantaged groups."

Discussion

1. In your own words, summarize each news broadcast.
2. Perform a news show in your class. Use broadcast items that deal with various current events.

LANGUAGE NOTES

Use of *Been to*

In the perfect tenses, *been* can be used as a past participle meaning *gone*. The two participles have different meanings, however. *Been* means "gone and returned," whereas *gone* does not carry the additional meaning of a return.

Examples:

Sheila has been to the art gallery. (She has returned.)

Ken has gone to the jogging track. (He has not come back yet.)

Have you ever been to Montreal?

No, I haven't been there before.

Complete the following sentences with either *been (to)* or *gone (to)*.

1. It's been a long day—Warren's _____ home.
2. That kid has _____ the corner store four times today.
3. The chairman of the Community League has _____ several political conventions in town.
4. Henry has _____ back to working as a political organizer.
5. Have you ever _____ Ottawa?

Voiced and Reduced *-t-*

A *t* between vowels or other voiced sounds is often voiced and reduced in informal speech. The resulting sound, called a "flap," sounds like a *d*, as in *butter*, *city*, *little*, and *letter*. The *d* sound makes pronunciation easier, but it does not occur when a person is speaking slowly or emphatically. The *t* sound also remains when it begins a stressed syllable, as in *return*. Those learning English need not use the *d* pronunciation, but it is helpful to recognize it.

Swearing

Swear words and their uses are often difficult to understand in a new language and culture. Translating or explaining swear words often poses problems; literal translations do not carry the same force as the original word. Different cultures use different kinds of words to express profanity. Religious words are used in Canadian French, for example, while animal words are often used in East European languages.

Generally, particular swear words lose their forcefulness over time and are replaced by other words. Words such as "damn," "hell," and "god" are often judged as mild today, whereas they brought a much stronger reaction fifty years ago.

A swear word may also have several, often milder, variations. "Heck" is a form of "hell," for example, and "darn" may be used for "damn." Other examples of mild replacements for swear words are: "fudge," "shoot," "fuddle-duddle," and "Holy Cow." These terms are often quite humorous.

Although some people commonly use swear words in their speech, swearing is not considered proper. It is better to avoid swear words than to use them and offend someone.

CULTURE NOTE

In Canada, there are three levels of government: municipal, provincial, and federal. At each level, voters elect their representatives by secret ballot. These representatives hold office for a specific length of time. For instance, provincial and federal representatives can hold their elected seats for up to five years before another election is called. Municipal officials hold office for a shorter period. Once given the mandate to govern, elected officials are responsible both for the smooth running of the government and for actively representing their constituents.

The Canadian parliamentary system is based on the British model. The House of Commons, for example, is made up of representatives who govern the country. The Senate, on the other hand, consists of members who are appointed by the Prime Minister. Moreover, the Canadian system allows for freely formed political parties in the House of Commons. There are three major political parties holding seats—the Liberals, Progressive Conservatives, and New Democrats. However, special interest groups, regional parties, and minor federal parties also exist in Canada.

Some Canadians find the political arena extremely fascinating; others find it boring. Involvement in politics can vary from active campaigning to simply voting during an election. In Canada, it is every citizen's right to vote. The ruling party is judged on its past performance and, in an election, can either be voted out or receive a fresh mandate. Canadians recognize their responsibility in choosing competent government and, as a result, their discussion of political issues can make for controversial conversations.

Additional Vocabulary

House of Commons—elected body that formulates laws

Senate—non-elected body that reviews new laws; it can delay legislation for a time, but the House of Commons is the final authority

M.P.—Member of Parliament

M.L.A.—Member of the Legislative Assembly (provincial government)

M.P.P.—Member of Provincial Parliament

Premier—leader of the provincial government

Charter of Rights—code outlining the rights and duties of Canadian citizens

mandate—political authority to act for the electorate

Discussion Topics

1. What do you think of news reporting in Canada? Is it informative and objective, for example?
2. Do you think government censorship of news items is necessary?
3. Identify some common uses of propaganda in the world.
4. Why is politics considered a controversial topic of conversation?
5. What political parties exist in your native country?
6. Compare political issues in Canada with those in your native country.

the Hansard

Activities

1. Organize a mock election in class. Have different students run for office and make campaign speeches.
2. Hold a debate on one of the following political issues:

   (a) The downtown core in our city must be revitalized.
   (b) Capital punishment should be reintroduced.
   (c) Universal family allowance payments should be discontinued.

Assignments

1. Using a phone book and other directories, make a list of useful government departments and organizations that you are unfamiliar with. Find out what they do and report to the class.
2. Identify a municipal, provincial, and federal politician and research his or her political background.

fifteen
The Marketplace

CUSTOMER SERVICE

(in a complaint department)

Employee: Good morning. May I help you?

Customer: Yes, I'd like a **refund** for this popcorn maker, please.

Employee: I'm sorry—sale items are non-returnable.

Customer: But this machine is **defective**. Look at it—it's all **scorched**.

Employee: What happened? Did you read the instructions before using it?

Customer: Of course I did. I read the booklet and followed the instructions exactly. But when I plugged it in, it started shooting popcorn kernels out all over the place. And then it started smoking, so I unplugged it.

Employee: It certainly does look burned out. Okay, I'll give you another unit and I'll send this one back to the manufacturer.

Customer: I think I'd rather have my money back. It made quite a mess and I don't want to risk that again.

Employee: Well, okay. I'll just check with the manager. In the meantime, could you please fill out this form?

Customer: All right.

refund—money paid back; reimbursement
defective—faulty, having something wrong with it
scorched—having a surface burn; discoloured from burning

Discussion

1. What is the policy for returning items at this store?
2. Practise variations on this dialogue with a fellow student. Try to get a refund for various household items that are defective, or that are the wrong size or colour.

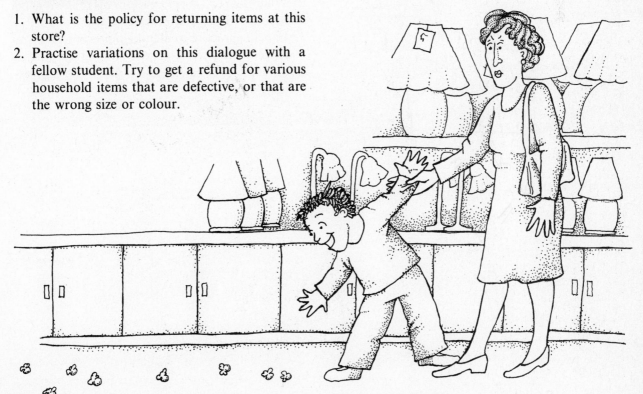

REDECORATING

bonus—extra pay given as a reward
sprucing up—(colloquial) fixing up
for a rainy day—(idiomatic) for an emergency, for later need
easy chair—armchair; big, comfortable chair

Mary:	Hey, honey, look—there's a big furniture sale on at Eaton's.
Hugh:	Furniture sale? What do we need with more furniture?
Mary:	Not more, new. We agreed to replace some of this old stuff if I got my **bonus**.
Hugh:	You want to replace these beautiful antiques?
Mary:	They're not antiques—they're junk. Look, this sofa sags in the middle, there are cat scratches on the drapes, and this armchair—well, even reupholstering won't help it.
Hugh:	Okay, okay. You've convinced me. This place could do with *some* **sprucing up**. Let's see that ad. Hmmm, 50% off, eh? We can even pay in monthly payments.
Mary:	But you always hate charging things. And we do have some money saved up **for a rainy day**, you know. I can at least start shopping around.
Hugh:	We can both do the shopping—it won't be easy finding a replacement for my favourite old **easy chair**.

Discussion

1. How does Hugh feel about buying new furniture?
2. What financial considerations make this a good time for Hugh and Mary to buy?
3. In pairs, practise similar dialogues in which one student tries to convince the other that a purchase of a new item for the house is necessary.

COMMERCIAL BREAKS

"Tired of **static cling**? Do your clothes come out of the dryer all stuck together? Is it a shocking experience? Try new improved Softie fabric softener. Your clothes will come out of the dryer soft and fluffy. No more annoying static cling. And the new April fresh scent will leave you thinking of the great outdoors. Buy new Softie today."

"This weekend only at Dizzy Dave's Discount Den—a special offer! No interest! No down payment! And twelve months to pay! Prices have been **slashed** on all living room and bedroom **suites**! 20% off all **VCR s** in the store! Don't miss this amazing sale!"

"**Mmmmm**, hot-out-of-the-oven muffins first thing in the morning? Sounds good—but no time to bake? No problem! New Bran Crunchie muffin mix is easy to make. Just add water and mix. Pour the batter into muffin tins, pop them into the oven, and **presto**! Fifteen minutes later you have hot delicious muffins. Even faster in a microwave. Start your day off right with the goodness of bran."

"What's her secret? She can't be a grandmother! She looks so young! You too can look young with Second Youth Skin Cream. Second Youth moisturizes your skin—helps keep those **tell-tale** wrinkles from forming. Your face will glow with youthfulness. Others will wonder what your secret is."

static cling—clothes sticking together because of electrical charges
slashed—cut drastically
suites—furniture combinations
VCR s—Video Cassette Recorders
mmmmm—(expression of delight) that's good
presto—suddenly, at once (term associated with magicians)
tell-tale—revealing information

Discussion

1. Explain each commercial in your own words. What is being sold? What are the advantages of the product?
2. What techniques are being used in the commercials to sell the products?
3. Describe a commercial that you find particularly effective. How is it effective? Is it humorous or annoying?
4. In small groups, develop your own television commercials. Perform them for the class.

LANGUAGE NOTES

Stress for Emphasis or Contrast

A stronger stress is given to words that need to be emphasized or contrasted in a sentence.

Examples:

Put that *on* the dresser, not *in* it.
I'm going, too.
He asked for the *red* lamp, not the blue one.
I do *not* want to hear about it.
Jane wrote that, not Chris.

Practise the following sentences, emphasizing the italicized word.

1. I'll buy *that* sweater, not the other one!
2. Don't forget, the letters have to be mailed by *5:00 p.m.*
3. She received a refund for the *popcorn* maker, not the coffee maker.
4. I do not want to hear *all* the details about your shopping trip!
5. Be careful! Don't buy a car that will be a *lemon*.

Use of *to Burn*

The verb *to burn* is completed by various prepositions depending on the subject of the verb. The past participle can be *burned* or *burnt*.

burn down—used for buildings destroyed to the foundations by fire
That factory burned down years ago.

burn out—used for buildings or vehicles where the shell still remains
That burnt out building should be knocked down; it's dangerous.

burn out—used for electrical appliances, candles, and matches that no longer work
Is the lightbulb burned out?

burn out—(idiomatic) used for people who are no longer able to work because of too much stress and over-work
With the pressures of the school system, there is a high incidence of teacher burn-out today.

burn up—used for most objects that are completely destroyed by fire
All the records were burned up in the fire.

burn up—(idiomatic) used for people who are angry
You mean he's late again? That really burns me up.

Place the correct idiom in the following sentences.

1. It_____ me _____ when I wait half an hour for him.
2. The lamps on the street _____ last night.
3. I'm afraid Laurie just couldn't handle social work; she _____ after six months.
4. An arsonist likes to _____ buildings.
5. The trees were all _____ in the forest fire.

CULTURE NOTE

North American culture is considered to be commercially oriented. Canadian consumers are constantly bombarded by various kinds of advertisements—in newspapers and magazines, on radio and television. Moreover, the choice of products in the marketplace can be overwhelming.

There are many ways for Canadian consumers to save money, however. Newspapers often contain advertisements for special sales and many businesses offer coupons and special deals. Second-hand stores and garage sales can also be a source of less expensive items. Shopping around can be time-consuming, but it is often rewarding.

Some say that North America is slowly becoming a cashless society. Credit cards, debit cards, and cheques make buying easy—too easy, perhaps. Many manufacturers who want the consumer to buy offer easy credit: "Buy now! Easy financing! No down payment!" By buying on installment, the consumer can have the product before he or she has actually saved the money for it; however, interest payments add substantially to the cost. "Plastic money" and easy financing often lead people to spend more than they can afford.

Although there are federal and provincial laws to protect the consumer from false advertising, high-pressure selling, and below standard products, it is still up to the careful consumer to avoid impulse buying and poor budgeting. Consumer groups test various products and publish lists of reliable products. Thus, the smart consumer is an educated one. There is a saying in Latin, *Caveat emptor*—"let the buyer beware."

Additional Vocabulary

deposit—sum of money paid as a pledge or promise to buy

warranty—guarantee from a manufacturer or store to repair or replace defective items, often with a specific time limit

scratch 'n dent sale—sale of items that are slightly damaged, usually with exterior imperfections that do not affect use

raincheck—promise that a customer can buy an out-of-stock item at a later date and for the price originally advertised

rip-off—(slang) bad deal, where someone has been taken advantage of or cheated

Discussion Topics

1. What kind of shopper are you? Do you like to shop? Are you a spendthrift or a penny-pincher (a spender or a saver)?
2. How do shopping practices here differ from those in your country, in terms of availability of merchandise, helpfulness of salespeople, financing, consumer protection, etc.?
3. What do you think is the best way to find a bargain?
4. What is your opinion of credit cards and other systems that replace cash?
5. Discuss the advantages and disadvantages of our commercially-oriented culture. What are some problems that consumers and business people face?

Activities

1. In pairs or small groups, develop and role play a dialogue dealing with different aspects of shopping, for example, a pushy door-to-door salesman, returning an item, or arranging financing.
2. In pairs, go through sales catalogues and pick out interesting items. Then role play a dialogue in which one partner argues that the item would be a perfect purchase, while the other argues that it is not worth purchasing.
3. Examine newspaper and magazine ads and radio and TV commercials. Analyze what makes them effective.

Assignments

1. Find out about the various consumer protection laws in your province or in the country.
2. Choose an expensive product, such as an appliance, and make a list of what you should look for before you buy it.
3. Using catalogues, make a list of possible gifts for a friend or family member on a special occasion, such as a birthday, Christmas, or a housewarming.

sixteen

On the Phone

PHONE CALLS

Many people dislike using the telephone, even though it is an essential part of modern life. Talking on the phone can be especially difficult for non-native speakers of English who often rely on visual cues. Telephone conversations, however, include several ritualized expressions. Learning these expressions, many of which are illustrated in the following dialogues, can make using the telephone less stressful.

1. *A:* Hello.
   B: Hi Joan. It's Margaret. Are you busy right now or do you have time to talk?
   A: Well, actually—I'm just on my way out the door to pick up Martin. Can I call you back this afternoon?
   B: Sure. I'll be in until five.
   A: Okay. Talk to you later.
   B: B'bye.

2. *A:* Hello.
   B: Hello. Is Roger there?
   A: No, I'm sorry. You must have the wrong number.
   B: Is this 555-7039?
   A: No, it isn't.
   B: Oh, I'm very sorry for bothering you. Good-bye.
   A: Bye.

3. *A:* Hello.
   B: Hello. Is Jonathan there, please?
   A: No, I'm sorry—he's not in right now. May I take a message?
   B: Yes, could you please tell him that Philip Masters called? He's got my number.
   A: Okay, I'll give him the message.
   B: Thank you. Good-bye.
   A: Bye.

4. *A:* Hello.
   B: Hello. Is Mr. Franklin in, please?
   A: Speaking.
   B: Good morning. I'm calling from Overleaf Bookstore. The book you ordered is in—*Modern English* by Marcella Frank.
   A: Fine—I'll come by and pick it up. Are you open Thursday evenings?
   B: Yes, until nine.
   A: Good. Thank you very much. Good-bye.
   B: Bye.

5. *A:* Hello.
   B: Good evening. This is Linda from Acme Carpet Sweepers. Your household has been selected for our special offer. You will receive a free gift and there is no obligation to purchase. One of our representatives will come by with your gift and will give you a demonstration of our new carpet care products . . .
   A: No, thank you. I'm really not interested.
   B: Are you sure? This gift will be yours to keep with no obligation.
   A: No, thank you. (firmly)
   B: All right then. Good-bye.
   A: Good-bye.

6. *A:* Hello.
   B: Hello, I'm calling about the freezer you have for sale. Is it still available?
   A: Yes, it is.
   B: Could you tell me more about it?
   A: Well, it's a small chest freezer, in excellent condition, only two years old, and we're asking $250 for it.
   B: Oh, actually I had something larger in mind. Thanks anyway. Good-bye.
   A: Bye.

7. *A:* Garneau Health Clinic. Please hold the line . . . Hello, sorry to keep you waiting. May I help you?
   B: Yes, I'd like to make an appointment to see Dr. Hillis.
   A: Is it for something urgent or just a regular visit?
   B: Just a check-up.
   A: Would Thursday, the 27th, at 2:15 be convenient?
   B: Yes, that's fine.
   A: May I have your name and phone number, please?
   B: Andrew Pearce, P-E-A-R-C-E. 555-8632.
   A: Have you seen Dr. Hillis before?
   B: Yes, I have.
   A: All right, we'll see you on the 27th then.
   B: Thank you. Good-bye.
   A: Bye.

8. *A:* Walden's Restaurant.
   B: Hello. I'd like to make reservations for dinner tonight. A party of four, at seven o'clock.
   A: Yes, that would be fine. And your name, please?
   B: Harrison.
   A: Fine, thank you, Mr. Harrison. We will see you then. Good-bye.
   B: Good-bye.

9. *A:* Department of Forestry.
   B: Yes, I'd like some information about permits for cutting Christmas trees.
   A: Just one moment. I'll connect you with the right office.
   B: Thank you . . .

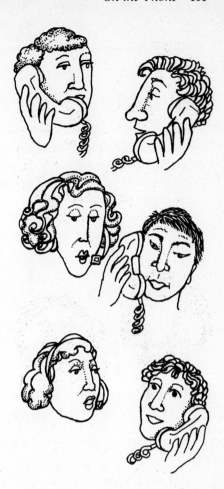

10. *A:* Directory Assistance. What city, please?
   B: Saskatoon.
   A: Thank you . . . Yes?
   B: I'd like the number for Murphy, M-U-R-P-H-Y, initial C.
   A: Thank you . . . Do you have an address for that name, sir?
   B: I think it's on Forest Avenue—I don't have the exact address.
   A: The number is 555-6047.
   B: 555-6047. Thank you.
   A: You're welcome.

11. *A:* Operator.
   B: Yes, I'd like to make a long distance collect call to Area Code 416, 555-0731.
   A: Thank you . . . May I have your name and number, please?
   B: 555-2498. Robert Peterson.
   A: Thank you . . . (ring, ring)
   C: Hello.
   A: I have a collect call from Robert Peterson. Will you accept the charges?
   C: Certainly . . . Hello, Bob . . .

LANGUAGE NOTES

Telephone Expressions

There are many common expressions used on the phone. For example, "Speaking" is the term used to acknowledge that you are the person asked for. "This is he" or "This is she" is sometimes used, but these phrases are quite formal.

Other commonly-used expressions include:

He's on another line right now. Would you like to hold?
She's not in right now. Can I get her to call you back?
You can reach him at 555-8242, extension 24.
I'd like some information on _____ .
Could you give me some information on _____?
Would you mind repeating that?
Could you repeat that, please?

To end a social call, common expressions are:

Well, I'd better let you go now.
It's been really nice talking to you.
I'm afraid I'm going to have to run.

Letters and Numbers

It is important to give information clearly on the telephone. Names often have to be spelled. Even common names in English have different spelling variations.

In spelling, it is important to pronounce the letters carefully. If there is a danger of misunderstanding the letter, a phrase, such as "M, as in Mother", can be used for clarification.

The names of the alphabet letters are similar in many languages and can be easily confused. Vowels, for example, can be difficult to distinguish, particularly "e" and "i." "J" and "g" can also be confused. In Canadian English, the last letter of the alphabet is usually pronounced "zed"; in American English, it is pronounced "zee."

Numbers also pose a problem. Check any numbers given by repeating them. Pairs such as "thirty" and "thirteen" are difficult for some people to distinguish. The "teen" numbers are pronounced with the stress on the second syllable. For example, compare:

thírty   thirteén

Note also that when a measurement is used as an adjective, the form becomes singular:

The boy is four years old.
He is a four-year-old boy.

The pipe is two metres long.
It is a two-metre pipe.

Practise the pronunciation of letters, numbers, and dates in class.

CULTURE NOTE

The following guidelines reflect telephone etiquette as understood by Canadians.

Residence phones are answered with a simple "Hello"; business phones are answered with the name of the business. An unidentified caller should not demand, "Who is this?" It is polite simply to ask for the person you are calling or to state the reason for the call. Do not identify yourself to an unknown caller and never give personal information on the phone. Some dishonest people use the phone to find out when a home will be unoccupied or to get credit card numbers.

It is important to get to the point quickly when you are making a telephone call. When calling for information, do not give a complete case history to the first person that answers the phone. State the nature of the call and be sure you are connected to the right person before going into details.

Be sure to repeat phone numbers and other information given over the phone. Do not be afraid to say, "I'm sorry. I didn't quite get that. Could you repeat the name, please?" If you don't understand a name given, ask for the spelling.

If you reach a wrong number, apologize politely. If you are not sure whether you mis-dialed or have the wrong number written down, check the number with the party you called. Do not ask for their number; give the number you wanted to call and ask for verification.

If a person is explaining something or giving information that requires a longer conversational turn, be sure to give occasional words of acknowledgement on the phone during the speaker's pauses. "Uh-huh" is used for a positive reaction; "uh-uh" is a negative one. If you are silent for too long, you will unnerve the speaker who will usually ask, "Are you still there?"

If an automatic answering machine takes your call, make sure you speak clearly and carefully, so that the message can be understood when the person plays back the tape. There are also answering services where a person will answer and take a message.

Canadians rely on the telephone, yet they often complain about it. For instance, many people dislike telephone solicitation (sales by telephone). Some people simply dislike talking on a phone. As well, rude callers, such as those who hang up the phone when an unfamiliar voice answers, can be very annoying. And for non-native speakers of English, the phone can be frightening.

A word about emergency calls:
Keep emergency phone numbers handy.

Do not call emergency phone numbers for information. Police and fire stations often have two numbers: one for emergencies and one for regular business.

If you require assistance (fire, police, ambulance), give your address right away. In the event that you are cut off, they will at least know where to find you.

Additional Vocabulary

Phrases describing the mechanics of a phone call:

—to look up a number in the phone book (or directory)
—to be on the line, on the phone
—to hang up at the end of a call
—to get a busy signal, the line is busy
—to dial the number (even with push-button phones)
—to be on hold
—to make a collect call, to reverse the charges
—to leave the phone off the hook
—to have a bad connection, static on the line
—a pay phone, a telephone booth

Discussion Topics

1. What do you notice about the way Canadians use the phone? Is it different in your culture?
2. What do you think of telephone solicitors?
3. Describe amusing experiences or problems that you have had on the phone.

Activities

1. Bring telephone books to class. Practise looking up various listings, in both the white and the yellow pages. Look up doctors, restaurants, taxis, and government offices for example.
2. In small groups, work on telephone dialogues. Practise the calls that you are most likely to make. Include emergency calls and calls for information.

Assignments

1. Make an information call at home. Use the yellow pages to find a business listing and then make the call and report to the class on your experience.
2. Keep a record of the telephone calls you receive in a week.
3. Find out about the various telephone services that are available both for private homes and for businesses.

Index of Language Notes

Index of Vocabulary Notes